KEYS TO BUYING FORECLOSED AND BARGAIN HOMES

Second Edition

Jack P. Friedman, Ph.D., C.P.A., M.A.I.
Real Estate Consultant
Dallas, Texas
and
Jack C. Harris, Ph.D.
Texas Real Estate Research Center
Texas A&M University
College Station, Texas

BARRON'S

Jack P. Friedman is a real estate consultant in Dallas, Texas. Jack C. Harris is a research economist at the Real Estate Center of Texas A&M University. They are the authors of *Keys to Investing in Real Estate, Keys to Mortgage Financing and Refinancing,* and *Keys to Purchasing a Condo or Co-op,* and Dr. Friedman is the author of *Keys to Buying and Owning a Home* in Barron's Business Keys Series.

All inquiries should be addressed to:
Barron's Educational Series, Inc.
250 Wireless Boulevard
Hauppauge, New York 11788
http://www.barronseduc.com

Library of Congress Catalog Card No. 99-59074

International Standard Book No. 0-7641-1294-5

Library of Congress Cataloging-in-Publication Data
Friedman, Jack P.
    Keys to buying foreclosed and bargain homes / Jack P. Friedman and Jack C. Harris. — 2nd ed.
        p. cm. — (Barron's business keys)
    Includes index.
    ISBN 0-7641-1294-5
    1. House buying.   2. Foreclosure.   3. Real estate investment.   I. Harris, Jack C., 1945–   .   II. Title.   III. Series.

HD1390.5.H36 2000
332.63'24—dc21

                                                                    99-59074

TABLE OF CONTENTS

1

GETTING A HOME
FOR A BARGAIN

A home is probably the biggest investment you will make in your lifetime. If you can get a quality property that serves your purposes and save money in the process, you will reap important financial benefits.

In a home purchase a bargain is one bought for less than its market value. However, a property's market value is not easy to determine because information about the market is incomplete and transactions are relatively infrequent. The lack of market information provides opportunities to buy below market value, but creates pitfalls as well. Sellers generally know what they own, including its problems. A property may be a bargain because an uninformed seller is asking too little, or is anxious or desperate to sell. It may be a bargain because it was foreclosed and the lender/owner is under pressure to sell it quickly. In such cases, the more you know about market value, the better off you are.

It is possible to save a good deal of money in a home purchase in other ways as well. Unlike many things you buy, a home does not have an established, take-it-or-leave-it price. Even new homes are subject to negotiation between buyer and seller before a selling price is set. And there are several things that add up to that "price." A seller may agree to pay all or some of the items at closing that buyers normally pay, such as legal fees, appraisal fees, or discount points on a loan. There may be concessions in the contract that potentially add value to the home. Seller financing may be part of the deal, the terms of which can be tailored to add value.

Obviously, understanding the bargaining process and what makes a property more valuable helps when you are trying to negotiate a favorable price. Even more important is how anxious each party is to make a sale. In markets where there are many buyers and few homes available, the seller can hold out for top dollar. But in cases where buyers are hard to find and there are plenty of homes on the market, the buyer can bargain. When the seller is under pressure to move the property, the result is often termed a "distress sale." By finding and sizing up such sales, a home buyer can save a great deal of money.

This book serves as a guide to finding and taking advantage of distress sale situations as well as other situations where there are opportunities to buy at below market price or with favorable financing. In most cases, distress sales follow when the property owner is in financial trouble and must sell the property. Many of these homes become foreclosed. Then the home generally goes into an inventory of repossessed homes, which eventually become available for sale. Holders of these homes may offer attractive deals to prospective buyers. The book explains the foreclosure process and how you can bid on homes at a foreclosure sale. Another section describes the types of holders of repossessed homes and how they go about liquidating these homes. Also included is a section on buying from these inventories. Many distressed properties are sold at auction, and a section details how a real estate auction works.

Distress properties may appeal to home buyers who thought they could never afford a home (there are some of these special programs for buyers with below-average incomes) and to real estate investors looking for good income-producing property. However, some of these properties are in poor condition or are located in areas that limit their value. This book will help you to evaluate an opportunity and to follow through once you decide on a course of action.

2

THE HOME BUYING PROCESS

If you've never bought a home before, you may not be familiar with the steps required to make the purchase or even how to get started. Even if you already own a home, you may want to use this Key to review the general procedure.

Buying a home in a distress sale may be quite different from the typical purchase procedure. However, to appreciate how it differs, you should know the "normal" procedure. (Virtually every home purchase turns out to be an adventure and requires some extraordinary action by the buyer, seller, or both. Nevertheless, there is a sequence of steps that most buyers and sellers attempt to follow.)

At some point in time, you come to the conclusion that your present housing is no longer satisfactory. You begin a search of the housing market to see what is available. This can be done in many ways. You may visit a **broker** and inspect the homes currently listed for sale. Most brokers are members of **Multiple Listing Services**, which means they can show you most of the homes currently for sale in the area. In addition, you can check ads in the paper or watch for "for sale" signs in the neighborhoods that most appeal to you. Home builders may conduct **open houses** and employ a sales staff to show you their subdivisions. You may access a web site of a real estate broker or local realtor's association to see what is on the market.

After making a preliminary search, you begin to form an idea of which areas, or specific homes, you like as well as how much house you can afford to buy. This latter point is important, since it makes no sense to consider homes you can't afford. A broker can work with you to determine your borrowing limit or you can visit a mortgage lender for the same purpose. The amount of loan you can get and how much it costs are determined by your income, credit history, and any long-term debts you now have.

Once you have decided on a specific home, you begin the negotiation process with the owner. Generally, this begins when you make an offer to buy the home for a certain price. In the purchase of real estate, verbal offers are worthless. To make a serious offer, you submit it using a form called a **binder** or **sales contract** and include a cash deposit (called **"earnest money"**). If your offer is below the price listed by the seller, and it usually is, the seller is likely to not accept your offer but instead return a **counter-offer**. This may continue until both sides are satisfied or negotiations break down. The contract describes the rights of both buyer and seller, so make sure that everything you need is stated, including a **closing date** at which time the property will be transferred.

After the contract is signed, you need to arrange financing. Approval usually takes from two to eight weeks, depending on the type of financing sought. You should have included a **contingency** in the sales contract so that if the financing you need cannot be arranged, the sale is called off and you can reclaim the earnest money. With a signed sales contract, you can make a formal application for a loan with a lending institution or mortgage banker. Some sales are made without such financing when the buyer **assumes** the existing loan or the **seller** provides the **financing**. The lender must determine the value of the property by hiring an appraiser and **qualify** the buyer for the amount of loan applied for. If the buyer is approved, the lender forwards the required money to the closing where it is distributed to the seller with set amounts going to other parties who are to receive a fee.

At the closing, all money is exchanged and title to the

property changes hands. Generally, a **title insurance company** is involved to assure that the buyer is receiving secure legal title to the property. There are various expenses, such as legal fees or real estate taxes, imposed upon either or both parties to the sale that are paid at closing. The closing marks the end of the home buying process.

3

WHAT IS FAIR VALUE?

There is a concept in economics called "market value." It is a theoretical concept based on having a large number of buyers and sellers competing with one another. The buyer willing to pay the highest price and the seller willing to accept the lowest price strike a deal. Other buyers aren't willing to pay so much or owners to accept so little at that moment. Also, the products are all the same (a bushel of wheat, for example), and the buyers and sellers are both informed and knowledgeable.

The real estate market doesn't work that efficiently. Each property is unique. Buyers and sellers don't get together in a central location such as a stock or commodities market. It may take months or years of exposure to the market before a property fetches market value. Yet the concept of market value is still used in real estate (see Key 49, Appraisals).

For distressed assets there is a concept of "fair value," set forth by the Office of Thrift Supervision (OTS), which differs from market value. Fair value is defined as "a method of determining what a troubled asset would be worth (its present value) if its present owner sold it in the current market." The OTS definition continues:

Fair value assumes a reasonable marketing period, a willing buyer and a willing seller. It assumes that the current selling price (its present value) would rise or fall in relation to the asset's future earnings potential. To calculate that price, fair value converts the asset's future earnings into what they are worth in today's dollars, using a formula that discounts the asset's future net cash flows. The discount is based on the fact that a dollar earned in the future is equal to, say, $.75 *invested today plus interest over an equivalent period of time. Thus, a dollar received today and invested is worth more than a dollar received in the future. Fair value, therefore, is based on a formula incorporating rates of interest earned. While market value measures the sales price agreed to by the buyer and seller, OTS defines fair value as measuring the value of what the seller would receive less selling costs. Fair value is one accounting method used to calculate the present value of an asset (a loan) at some point after the loan has become past due and book value is no longer valid.*

As a buyer seeking a bargain, or as a seller who is "motivated," you might think of "fair value" as the amount to be paid or received, rather than the higher "market value."

4

CAN YOU GET A BARGAIN HOME?

To get a bargain, you must be willing to spend the time and effort to become familiar with the market and investigate the property. Most people seeking foreclosed or distress sale property are hoping to get a good property at a steal. Some buyers indeed get exceptional values, taking advantage of situations that favor buyers and being in the right place at the right time. Others end up with properties that have more problems than expected, and eventually require so much additional investment that they, too, lose the homes to foreclosure. Then there are those who lose sight of why they are trying to buy a foreclosed home and pay too high a price in the competition to win the bidding.

The key to getting a bargain is knowing what you are getting and understanding what its value is in the market. Making "low ball" bids on any property available will probably not be successful. When it does work, you may be getting a property with so many problems that no other bidder was interested.

Most properties are offered "as is," but you have the opportunity to inspect the property before making a bid. You should always take advantage of this opportunity, even to the extent of hiring a professional inspector for properties you are serious about. Further, do your homework. You should consider the neighborhood, especially how it influences the value of the property and how appropriate it is for the use you intend. If the property is surrounded by other vacant buildings, understand that you are gambling on recovery of the area at some time in the near future. Any risk that you are forced to take should be reflected in the price you offer.

You should always have a reference value to compare against the price you are prepared to pay for the property. The reference should be a comparable property in what you consider to be acceptable condition. You can estimate what it would take to make the property you are considering equal to the reference property. This amount should be deducted from the reference value when deciding on your "reservation price."

Your reservation price is the highest you should be willing to pay for the property. Consider the prices of other properties in the market, likely future opportunities to buy other properties, and how badly you want this one. Decide what price would be the most you would pay if you really had to. That amount is your reservation price. Write it on a piece of paper and do not allow yourself to pay more. You hope you can get the property for something less than your reservation price. If so, you may have gotten a true bargain. But never pay more than your reservation price even though it means not "winning" the bid.

You may even want to have an appraisal done on the property (see Key 49). This will tell you what comparable properties have sold for recently. The cost of the appraisal ($300–$400) can be worth it if it keeps you from making a costly error and paying too much for the property. Another approach is to include in the contract that the house must appraise for at least the amount you agree to pay. If it appraises for less than the contract, you can negotiate a lower price or walk away from the deal.

Holders of foreclosed homes are receiving little or no benefit from keeping the property in inventory. Therefore, they should be anxious to sell. However, they do want to get as high a price as possible. They may be willing to hold the property rather than sell it for less than they consider obtainable in the market. Sometimes you can get a bargain if you quickly satisfy what the holder needs. That may mean having the cash or pre-arranged financing to swing the deal. It may mean being able to complete the transaction without delay.

5

BUYING FOR INVESTMENT VERSUS HOMEOWNERSHIP

How you approach foreclosed real estate depends on whether you are looking for a property to live in or to rent out. To some extent, your situation will have a lot to do with whether you should consider distressed property at all.

When you buy a property to be your home, your primary concern is whether the property can provide the type of home environment you want. First, you want to locate in an area that is relatively convenient to your place of work and other areas you visit frequently. You want a neighborhood that is reasonably secure and a good place to raise a family or to do whatever your personal life style entails. In general, an area where homeowners keep their properties in good order and where industrial, commercial, and heavy traffic is at a minimum helps protect the value of your investment. Finally, the home itself should be attractive and provide enough space for your needs.

For investment property, your focus is different. You want a property that can be rented for enough to cover expenses and provide some return. Only under special circumstances should you rely on appreciation in value to provide a return on your investment. The property should provide "cash flow"—that is, rental income must exceed out-of-pocket costs. Look for factors that might make it hard for you to keep the property rented. These include undesirable features that drive away tenants or cause a lot of turnover. For example, a high crime area would repel good tenants and leave you with those to whom you might not want to rent. If the neighborhood is not well kept, the value of your property may decline unless the opportunity arises to convert to another use.

If you are buying a house that will be your home, you may be coming to the transaction with extra baggage. You may currently be obligated on a lease or own a home that must be sold before you can buy the new home. If this is the case, you may not be in a good position to bid for foreclosed property. Many sellers will not entertain offers contingent on the sale of other property. If you require approved financing, you face a handicap in competing with other buyers. Finally, many properties are offered "as is," and you may not be able to get a guarantee of good working order.

As an investor, on the other hand, you are probably in a better position to deal. However, you must still do your homework before negotiation and be ready to make a solid offer when an opportunity arises. You may even be able to identify several acceptable properties. Then you can go for the one that turns out to represent the best value. In that way, you will be less likely to overpay because you became wedded to one property.

A good approach to use as an investor is to determine whether the property will provide a cash flow. You can figure how much the monthly payments will be, and see whether rent will cover them. For example, suppose you will have the following monthly payments:

Principal and Interest	$500.
Taxes	75.
Insurance	50.
Repairs, painting, maintenance	75.
Monthly requirements	$700.

If the property is not expected to rent for more than $700, you better pass it up because you will experience negative cash flow. Buy it only if it is likely to appreciate in value or provide other benefits in the future.

(For more on real estate investing, see Barron's *Keys to Investing in Real Estate.*)

6

A WORD ABOUT RISK

"Risk" is a peculiar word with many connotations. Generally, it is thought to represent the possibility of taking a chance on an event that could cause a loss. Flying in an airplane, riding in a car, or even crossing a street is thought by some to have some risk, albeit a minimal one. Some people define risk as the bad side of a chance and reward as the good side; hence, the term risk/reward is used.

In business, *risk* may be defined as representing both good or bad. Drilling for oil is risky: you'll make money with a hit, lose money with a miss. So the risk goes in both directions.

In buying a house you take several risks:

1. Physical condition
2. Future value
3. Interest rates
4. Rental rates
5. Liquidity/marketability
6. Future events

You can try to take steps to minimize risk, including due diligence (study before buying) and insurance.

Physical condition. The physical condition of a house is important. Investigate its structural soundness, electrical and mechanical systems, and need for repairs. There are professional house inspectors who can help. An inspector can determine whether the house has contaminants such as asbestos (preferably remove it or encapsulate it), lead-based paint, urea formaldehyde insulation, or underground storage tanks (remove). Disclosure laws require sellers to tell what they know.

Inspectors can test for radon in the air or water; they can find out whether the house has experienced water damage or a fire.

Future value. Will the house appreciate or decline in value? Because real estate is a prisoner of its location, it is important to investigate the neighborhood. Is it declining, stable, or on the upswing? Is the local and national economy weak or strong? Is the neighborhood dependent on one major employer? If so, is that employer and its industry healthy? Generally, a diversified economy is preferred. If the area is growing, what is the likelihood of its experiencing overbuilding that would depress prices?

Interest rates. These have an extensive effect on real estate. Rising rates may stop or slow new construction and may negatively affect your ability to resell. Falling interest rates could be a sign of economic weakness. Lower rates may provide an opportunity for you to refinance and reduce the payments, although there are costs involved.

Rental rates. Economic conditions may cause rental rates to rise or fall. You will need to achieve a certain rent just to break even (pay interest and operating expenses). Determine what occupancy rate and rental rate you need to break even, and get a good sense of how likely that is to be achieved. If the rent is not enough to break even, then you will need another financial benefit, such as appreciation in value, to justify the purchase.

Liquidity/marketability. Can this property be resold easily and quickly? Get a sense of how easily it can be marketed, especially if there is a possibility that you will need to sell unexpectedly or in a hurry. The amount of sales activity in the market is an indicator of liquidity.

Future events. Although we can't predict the future, try to envision what might happen down the road. Is the home on a busy or noisy street that is worsening? Or is it in a quiet, stable neighborhood? Is it in a hurricane-prone area, a flood plain, or near a geological fault line? Have many storms or earthquakes hit the area through the years? Do the houses have wood shingle roofs that are prone to fires? Are these risks insurable? At what cost? Although we can't protect against all risks, avoid properties that bring more risk than you care to assume. And even if a risk is insurable, there is an expense to insure, plus plenty of inconvenience if the event occurs.

7

RECOGNIZING A BUYERS' MARKET

A big part of getting a bargain in any market is buying when market conditions favor buyers over sellers. This occurs when sellers are relatively competitive but buyers are not. When there are a lot of people wanting to sell houses compared to the number of willing buyers, sellers have to be much more accommodating if they wish to be successful. In fact, it is the anxious or desperate seller that bargain-conscious buyers seek out.

When buyers have the upper hand in negotiations, the market is said to be a "buyers' market." The classic buyers market features a lot of sellers who must sell, mainly because they must move to another city or they need the sale to complete a purchase of a bigger home. At the same time, buyers have a lot of discretion about what and when they purchase. They can afford to wait until the price is right.

Of course, the opposite situation also occurs. A "sellers' market" exists when there are a lot of buyers who need a home while sellers have the discretion to wait for the best price. In a sellers' market, it is not unusual for sellers to receive more than one offer on a home shortly after it is exposed to the market. Obviously, in such a situation, few true bargains will be found (although it might be possible in certain "turnaround" neighborhoods).

In a buyers' market, conditions may not appear very favorable for investment. The city may be losing population and struggling economically. Mortgage loans may be hard to find. The thing to keep in mind is that these conditions are likely to change over time. The seeds of many real estate empires were sown during the depression of the 1930s when prices were low, loans were scarce, and people were trying to unload property. The people who had cash, access to capital, and the foresight to buy real estate eventually ended up with excellent investments.

Here are some things to look for that may indicate a buyers' market:

- Concentrations of "for sale" signs, particularly when the broker's name changes every three to six months. In depressed markets caused by the closure of a major employer, whole neighborhoods may go on sale as people are forced to move for economic reasons.
- Newspaper stories about layoffs and indications of local businesses shutting down.
- Reports of high mortgage foreclosure rates. A preliminary sign of rising foreclosures is the loan delinquency rate (the percentage of loans in which payments are one to three months in arrears). Information on delinquency rates for many metropolitan areas can be purchased from the Mortgage Bankers Association at www.mbaa.com.
- Widespread evidence of price markdowns. Advertisements will report "price reduction," or similar language. Overpriced real estate can occur in any market, but in a depressed market, overpricing will be common, simply because sellers were getting those prices before the slump.
- Lots of open houses. In a slow market, agents will be trying every tactic available to drum up business.
- Lack of new construction. When markets begin to slow, a lot of new homes will come to market. There is a tendency for construction to lag the market cycle. Builders are encouraged when the market peaks, but it takes time to produce new homes. Therefore, a lot of production shows up too late. This added supply tends to further soften the market

When few buyers materialize to absorb the new supply, the flow will stop. This is a signal that the time is right for bargain hunting.

- Auctions. In this country, real estate auctions often are a sign of distressed property. When auctions become a common event, it probably means that sales through traditional means are difficult. At the same time, large inventories of repossessed real estate often are offered at an auction.
- Unfavorable terms on mortgage loans. In slow markets, the collateral value of real property is lessened. Faced with rising foreclosures, lenders are not as enthusiastic about making new loans. Consequently, they make only the ones with the lowest risk, meaning those with low loan-to-value ratios, high discount points, and tough qualifying criteria. A buyers' market favors those with top-notch credit ratings and ample cash.

It is important to understand that a market might not be a pure buyers' or sellers' market, but may be anywhere on the scale between these extremes. You may not find all the characteristics listed above, but conditions should be more in the direction described than the opposite. Any tendency toward these conditions will favor the buyer.

Likewise, if you buy in a buyers' market, do not expect to make a quick profit by turning the property over. When you go to sell, the market is working against you, unless the cycle quickly reverses. It may take anywhere from two to eight years for the market to shift. If you are buying for personal use, this probably will not be a problem, because the average holding period for owner-occupied homes is seven to ten years. If you intend to rent out the home, you may have to endure several years of high vacancy and poor rent production before demand recovers. The bargain-conscious investor must be prepared to endure such periods. In fact, this may be a time when additional investment is required to upgrade your ability to find decent tenants.

Finally, there is a chance that, instead of the market cycling, it actually is in irretrievable decline. If this is the case, the value of the property will not recover, but will only decrease. This rarely happens with whole cities (there is such a thing as a ghost town, formed when the one economic activity that created a boom town suddenly shuts down), but it may happen to specific areas of a city. Look for things that indicate fundamental change in how the neighborhood is used. For example, if homes in the area are being converted to commercial use, it could mean value decline for the properties that remain residential. Physical conversion of single-family homes to apartments and group quarters is another sign of permanent change. In these instances, the "bargain" home may actually be fairly priced, or even overpriced.

8

BUYING OUT OF SEASON

One way to improve your chances of getting a good price on a home is to buy at the right time of year. Home prices tend to show what economists call "seasonal variation." In other words, there is a consistent pattern in home prices that appears year after year. The chart shows how median home prices, as reported by the National Association of Realtors®, have varied by month over the years 1994–98.

EXHIBIT 1

Home Prices Tend to Change According to Season

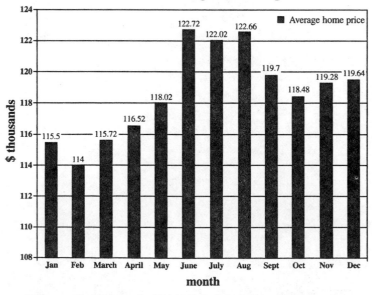

*Average median home price for 1994–98, National Association of Realtors®.

As shown, prices tend to peak in the summer and to be lowest in the winter. The main reason for this pattern is the greater number of home buyers in the market during the late spring and early summer months. Keep in mind that the data shown are for closings, so the price reported in any one month reflects a transaction that was agreed upon from a few weeks to several months earlier. With more competition for the homes on the market, prices rise. This is sort of a mini-version of the longer range change from a buyers' to sellers' market. Consider the spring and summer to be "mini-sellers' markets."

Likewise, the winter may be a better time to buy; a mini-buyers' market, in a sense. There are fewer buyers competing for homes. Why the variation in buyers from season to season? Some of it has to do with the reasons people move, and, thus, buy a home. Job transfers can occur in any season, but employees who have some say in the decision often prefer to relocate during the summer. The same goes for those who are moving to improve their housing situation. Conditions are more pleasant for house hunting and for moving during the spring. Many families with school-age children try to time a move so as not to disrupt the school year. The children do not have to be uprooted from one school to another while classes are ongoing.

Likewise, house buying and moving are to be avoided at year end. Notice in the chart that prices tend to rise a bit at the end of the year, after a big decline in the fall. Some of this rise is merely the tendency for prices to rise over time regardless of season. But some of the rise may reflect the desire of some buyers to reward themselves with a special Christmas present of a new home.

At any rate, the best time to get a bargain appears to be during the first few months of the year. One possible down side to this strategy, aside from the rigors of touring homes during the winter, is the reduction in the number of homes on the market at that time of year. After all, most people put their home on the market because they, themselves, are buying a new home. Therefore, some of the same timing dynamic works on the supply side as well as the demand side. So, you may not find the same variety of choices as you might later in the year. On the other hand, if your strategy is to find the most motivated sellers, you will probably have more luck in the winter. Many of these homes either sat on the market during the previous year without being sold or the sellers got into the market too late. Either way, the reality of knowing they are not in the best negotiating position will make sellers much more receptive to low, but reasonable, offers.

9

FOR SALE BY OWNER

With real estate brokerage commissions in the 5 to 7 percent range, some homeowners, in an effort to "avoid the middleman," will sell the home themselves at a discount, effectively passing the "savings" to the buyer. In most cases, you shouldn't expect to get the entire discount. After all, the seller is taking on the work of making a sale. Negotiating somewhere in the middle can still provide a bargain price.

There is also a possibility that an owner has mis-priced his or her home and is offering it for sale far below its market value. Be prepared to move quickly when you spot a bargain for sale by owner (FSBO or "fizz-bo") because others may do the same. There are sellers, as well, that have an inflated impression of the value of their property. They list high and refuse to come down. Pass these by, as they probably will be a waste of time.

Although some owners are intimidated by the thought and process of selling a house, others are not. They simply would rather not deal with a broker. They know that lawyers and title companies will assure transfer of legal title and avoid ownership minefields. Should you "low ball" these sellers, making an extremely low offer in hopes of getting a maximum bargain? Only if you are not seriously considering the property, but would buy it at a rock bottom price. When dealing directly with a seller, it is important to go out of your way not to anger the person if you truly want to negotiate a deal. A person selling a home may have some emotional involvement in the process.

There are even real estate brokers who are geared to help sellers sell on their own. Some brokers specialize in helping owners do everything themselves. They provide a kit with a yard sign, sample contracts to complete, and help for the seller at a flat fee or low percentage rate. Typically, they do not advertise or show the house, though those services can be contracted at additional cost. There even is the beginning of a type of Multiple Listing Service for FSBOs using the Internet.

Dealing directly with an owner can be effective. There will not be a broker to interpret or misinterpret a spoken statement or intent. Closing, possession, and moving dates can be arranged face-to-face, without a middleman trying to recall exactly what his principal said. On the other hand, without a broker acting as a buffer, words can be misinterpreted as too harsh, causing the proposed deal to fall through. Be prepared to deal with inexperienced sellers by having your own contract forms, including the disclosures required in many states. You will have to be prepared to do all the things a buyer needs to do prior to closing, such as making sure that inspections are made and the financing is ready.

The matter of holding the deposit money can be a problem. Do not give the money directly to the seller. Get a trusted third party, such as a title company, to do this. The deposit is then applied in accordance with the contract, according to the title company's interpretation of the contract.

An attorney and/or title company will be used in the sale of any home. The absence of a broker should not adversely affect a knowledgeable, experienced buyer who gets help from an appraiser, home inspector, or lender. The lender will not finance the purchase of a house that is overpriced or has serious legal flaws. Therefore, the feeling of security one may get from a broker's involvement is often brought about by others in the transaction. In some circumstances, the absence of a broker can simplify the buying process as well as provide you with a bargain.

10

WHY THE LOW PRICE? SELLER, HOUSE, OR NEIGHBORHOOD

When buying a foreclosed or bargain house, you must be especially mindful of the reason for its attractive price. Three major possibilities exist for a low price:

1. An anxious, motivated, or ignorant seller
2. Poor physical condition of the house
3. Problems in the neighborhood

The seller. Ideally, you want a house where something has gone wrong with the seller. This may sound a little callous, but keep in mind that by buying out the interest of someone who is in over their head is actually a beneficial thing. The seller may be a private individual or family who is ignorant of price, needs to sell quickly, or has little at stake in the price. It may be an institution that has foreclosed or a relocation company. Someone else will absorb the loss from a quick sale. After you buy, prior owners go away, so you will hope there is nothing wrong with the house itself or its neighborhood.

The house. The house may have adverse physical characteristics that cause a problem. It could be a poorly built new house (substandard labor and materials) or a functionally obsolete older house (no insulation, too few bathrooms, inadequate wiring or plumbing, no provision for off-street parking of two cars). It may be in need of physical repairs—for example, replacement of floor coverings or window treatments, paint inside and out, facade repair, roof replacement, or structural repair.

It may need costly electrical or plumbing repair.

To determine whether such a house is a bargain, start with the estimated market value if everything were in good condition; then subtract the cost of repairs. Houses are generally repairable—at some cost.

The neighborhood. Unlike sellers (whom you may never see again) or houses (generally repairable), there is nothing you can do about the neighborhood. If the neighborhood is in a downward trend, stay away. The downturn may be evidenced by a high rate of crime, serious crimes, low-scoring schools, poor area employment prospects, high unemployment rates, very low-income levels, or a high proportion of residents living in substandard or public housing. At some future time, conditions may improve—but you might not be able to wait that long, and you can exercise no control over the neighborhood.

Instead, look for a stable or improving neighborhood. This will have a high percentage of owner-occupied homes, average or better schools, low crime rates, and steady or strong employment in the region.

Employment is important for two reasons:

1. People want to live in places where there is economic opportunity.
2. Jobs provide the local area with income to spend on housing and other goods.

The employment opportunities need not be within the immediate neighborhood; preferably within an easy commute, either by car or, in the case of low- or moderate-income areas, by public transportation.

When employment prospects are bleak because a major employer or industry has closed or moved, housing prices will decline. Whether they are a bargain depends on prospects for recovery. If the economic downturn is temporary or cyclical, bargains can be had. But beware of permanent declines.

11

WHY SOME HOMES ARE UNDERVALUED

Some houses may sell for less than others in the neighborhood because they possess one or more undesirable features. If you are buying it for the long term and plan to rent it to a tenant, such a house may be perfectly acceptable. Renters may not be as fussy as buyers. In fact, a feature such as being on a bus line could be a positive factor for a renter, whereas a buyer might prefer to avoid the busy street. So, as a buyer-investor, you might seek out houses that are appreciated more by renters than by potential buyers.

Low prices may result from factors in these general areas:

1. Physical depreciation
    * Short-lived assets
    * Long-lived assets
2. Functional obsolescence
3. Economic/external obsolescence

See if you can identify the principal reasons why the house you recently visited hasn't sold and whether it is undervalued or priced correctly when you take the defect(s) into account. Flaws could fall into any of the following categories:

Physical depreciation—short-lived assets: paint, carpet/floor covering, wallpaper, curtains, furnace/air conditioning, appliances, and roof covering.

Physical depreciation—long-lived assets: studs, underground piping, foundation walls, and insulation.

Functional obsolescence (depending on tastes in the

area): absence of air conditioning, carport or single car garage, poor floor plan, inadequate wiring, small rooms, too many or too few bathrooms, outmoded kitchen, and ceilings too low or too high.

External economic or environmental obsolescence (from outside the property): nearby noise from traffic or trains, pollution, commercial property, nuisances, eyesores, overhead wires, substandard schools, and substandard municipal services.

There is no such thing as a perfect house. The idea is to buy one at a bargain price that is likely to appreciate through the years.

12

INSPECTING THE PROPERTY

You should always inspect a property thoroughly before making an offer. When you are buying repossessed property, such an inspection is even more important, since it may be difficult or impossible to insert an addendum into the sales contract to cover repairs. In addition, many repossessed homes have sat vacant for extended periods (some may even have been vandalized by their previous owners) and may need repairs and remedial upkeep. You will want to know about such conditions before you bid because the condition of the property will affect how much you bid or even if you bid at all.

Since you are concerned about what a property is worth—even if the home is ideally suited to you, there is no need to bid more than market value—you should inspect the property from the viewpoint of an appraiser. This means you want to look at several different factors that affect the property's market value. The most logical way to approach this is to start with the more general and move to the specific. This also provides the advantage of allowing you to screen out properties without going through an entire analysis. In fact, at the more general levels, you can consider more than one property at a time.

Let's say that you want to invest locally and have settled on the general area. You should develop some idea of what neighborhoods are the most desirable for the type of property you want to own. You should check out the location from the standpoint of how convenient it is to employment centers and other areas of interest. This should be evaluated from the viewpoint of your lifestyle (if you plan to occupy the home) or that of your prospective tenants (if you plan to rent out the home). For example, access to public transportation may be important for college students or the elderly.

Next look at the residential quality of the neighborhood. Is it attractive? Is there too much traffic? Are there conveniently located parks? Do people maintain their homes well? Does the area appear to be changing in its use (encroaching commercial uses, vacant buildings, conversions of single-family homes to apartments)? The home you are considering may be in excellent condition. However, a deteriorating neighborhood will frustrate the best maintenance program. As an individual homeowner, there is little you can do about it.

Look at how the property fits into the neighborhood. Is there a great amount of conformity? Do surrounding homes have features that the subject lacks, or vice versa? In general, it is better to be deficient (and pay less) if the home can be brought up to the area standards without great expense. Adding features that are uncommon to the neighborhood will do little to improve the value of the home.

Finally, examine the home. You may want to employ a professional home inspector to help you at this stage. The inspector will check out the plumbing, mechanical, and electrical components of the home and point out any deficiencies and defects. You may need a second inspector, a structural engineer, for the foundation. A good inspector should be able to find things that may take you several years to discover. Make a list of things that can be repaired economically and things that would cost too much to do (such as changing an awkward floor layout). You can estimate the cost of doing the repairs and the reduced value of putting up with those features that cannot be changed.

In addition to the physical inspection, it is worthwhile to check the public record for any outstanding taxes. Any back taxes due the city, county, school district, other governmental unit carry over to the new owner. The same is true of homeowner association dues and assessments that have not been paid. Failure to make these debts good can result in loss of property when the government liens are enforced.

This information will be helpful when you are preparing a bid (see Key 25). It may be that you can avoid bidding at all, if the property is not suitable or has too many problems. In fact, you may write off entire neighborhoods based on your initial evaluations.

13

WINNING WITH REPOSSESSED HOMES

Possibly the ultimate motivated seller is the one who acquired the home as a consequence of a failed business agreement. Such is the case of lending institutions, mortgage insurance companies, and others who stand behind the borrower's obligation to repay the loan. When the borrower defaults, one of these institutions likely will end up with the property.

These entities acquire properties to try to recover their investment in the loan. Their hope is to liquidate the property as soon as possible for enough to repay the loan principal, accrued interest, and expenses of recovery. Time is of the essence, in most cases. They tend to be very cooperative with the interested buyer. Typically, they have processes in place for accepting bids and occasionally place properties at auction.

Among these institutions are those that hold mortgages. Some are depository institutions, such as banks and savings and loan associations, that originate loans and hold them in portfolio. When a borrower defaults, the lender may foreclose the loan and either take over the property in a nonjudicial foreclosure or purchase the property at a foreclosure sale held as part of a judicial foreclosure. Similarly, mortgage investors may acquire properties when the mortgages they hold are foreclosed. The biggest mortgage investors are the federally sponsored organizations of Fannie Mae and Freddie Mac.

Many mortgage loans require mortgage insurance that protects the lender in the case of borrower default. When such insurance is in effect, the insuring or guaranteeing organization generally acquires the property after foreclosure. These organizations include private mortgage insurers, such as the Mortgage Guaranty Insurance Corporation (MGIC), the Federal Housing Administration (FHA), or the Veterans Administration (VA). Also, the Federal Deposit Insurance Corporation (FDIC), which insures deposit accounts in banks and savings and loans, acquires properties in the course of liquidating failed lending institutions.

Anyone interested in bargain properties should become familiar with the procedures required to buy from these organizations. Often, the properties are marketed under listing contracts, just like most other properties on the market. Therefore, one avenue to explore is inquiries with local real estate agents. Holders of large inventories of properties will have methods by which a prospective buyer can place bids on properties. Often, sealed bids are accepted over a specific period of time and the best qualifying bid is accepted. Other Keys in this book provide more detail on how each of the major holders of repossessed homes operates.

There are several advantages of buying homes through these procedures:

- In many cases, the properties have been upgraded to comply with local codes or to the standard required to get financing or insurance from the selling institution. Buyers, however, should always inspect the properties prior to committing. (One caveat in dealing with repossessed property is that the institutions and firms that sell these homes are not subject to the property condition disclosure requirements that apply to individual sellers.)
- Some sellers offer financing, often at favorable terms. In this way, the holder of the property hopes to turn a bad debt into a new performing loan. Unless you plan to pay cash, the opportunity to get financing can be valuable.
- Organizations with government ties, such as the

FHA, Fannie Mae, and Freddie Mac, may have special deals for certain types of buyers or for homes in certain locations. For example, some give priority to buyers who plan to occupy the home, to first-time home buyers or to those bidding on homes in depressed neighborhoods.

- Some sellers may be willing to pay a portion of the closing costs normally paid by the buyer.

Although institutions are highly interested in getting rid of these properties, they are not panic sellers. They are not willing to give them away. Usually, they will try to get all or a large proportion of what they have invested in the property. If the bids are not high enough, they may wait for better ones to come in. It is important to do the homework required to fairly price the properties. If you want to bid low, in hopes of getting the best price, you should be prepared to lose out most of the time. Usually, if the organization wants a quick sale, it will call an auction for a group of properties. Even then, it may place a reservation price to try to limit its loss. The bidder should know the market price and the procedures of the organization offering the property.

14

SNATCHING A HOME FROM THE JAWS OF FORECLOSURE

Foreclosure is almost always a financial catastrophe for the homeowner and often presents the lender with a loss as well. Therefore, it is in everyone's interest to avoid the event. The homeowner will try to sell the home when facing difficulties in keeping up payments. However, if the sale will not yield enough money to pay off the loan, most financially strapped homeowners have little choice than allowing foreclosure to proceed.

Knowing that foreclosure sales rarely cover the outstanding loan and expenses, lenders sometimes will try to work out a solution with a homeowner who wishes to keep the home and retains some ability to support a loan. Such a work-out may involve restructuring the loan to provide lower monthly payments or even accepting a reduced pay-back.

When a lender is willing to be flexible to revive a loan, there may be an opportunity for a third party, you, to forge an attractive deal. This is particularly the case when the present homeowner clearly has no ability or intention to retain the home. You may step into the homeowner's place and break the roadblock to working out a solution that avoids foreclosure.

Such situations will not be widespread, even when foreclosures are running at above-normal levels. Many loans are held in institutional pools that may preclude any type of work-out that lowers their value. In any case, you would need to step in before foreclosure had begun.

The key to identifying such cases is a knowledgeable broker who works with homeowners and is aware of the possibilities of a pre-foreclosure sale. If you are interested in such opportunities, inform a broker you have confidence in that you might be willing to be party to a work-out under the right terms. It will not be surprising if the broker has several current cases of homeowners faced with the likelihood of foreclosure. However, the broker must also be willing to contact the lender and sound out the possibilities of a work-out. Another source is classified ads in the newspaper where individuals may advertise for sale by owner (FSBO). Individual owners may also plant a "for sale" sign in their yard. It is worth a call to get more information and a feel for the market.

Before entering into negotiations, there are some bits of information you should gather. Of course you should inspect the property to see whether it is suitable for your lifestyle, just as in any other purchase. Determine your maximum price based on comparable properties and, if you intend to rent out the home, what price will be low enough to allow rent to provide a reasonable return. Make sure the loan that is being restructured is the only lien against the property. You do not want to be surprised by a bill for delinquent taxes or homeowner association dues or find out later that a second mortgage exists. Find out the terms on the existing loan and whether the lender can and will allow it to be assumed. If not, you may have to arrange outside financing. In most cases, the lender will prefer restructuring the financing if the price is right, since this may avoid the necessity of devaluing the loan on the lender's books.

A mutually beneficial match on a pre-foreclosure sale may be hard to find. However, when it does occur, it can be extremely beneficial. Think of yourself as providing the key to a win-win solution for both the lender and homeowner. But do it only if the deal also works to your benefit.

15

BANKS DON'T WANT TO OWN REAL ESTATE

Banks and other lending institutions are not prepared to own real estate. Their daily business is shuffling money and papers—not managing property. Their staff has a daily routine that consists of taking deposits and making loans. When it comes to the ownership, management, and resale of foreclosed properties, they are lacking in staff, expertise, and resources. That is why foreclosure is considered a last resort, and why banks are anxious to rid themselves of foreclosed houses.

Banks must continually meet tests conceived by government regulators and applied by auditors or examiners to show they have adequate capital to operate safely. Owning real estate other than their own buildings, called real estate owned (REO) or loans through foreclosure (LTF), is counterproductive to meeting capital tests, to the growth of their bank, and to smooth operations. Generally, bank personnel are rewarded for making good loans and servicing the loans. Owning repossessed real estate is a drag on their operations and growth. Loan officers will not be rewarded for having an inventory of foreclosed property. If bank personnel work with foreclosures, any reward will be for the quick disposal of foreclosed property, which could mean quick sales at low prices.

If you are interested in acquiring a portfolio of foreclosed houses at bargain prices, then meet and make friends with the bankers in charge of these assets at various banks in your city or town. Ask the banker to call you when a property has been or is about to be foreclosed.

Try to keep a checking or savings account at each bank. Often you will need friends or relationships at several banks because each may have a policy preventing them from financing properties that they have foreclosed but allowing them to finance others' property coming out of foreclosure. That is, you need one bank to buy from and a different one to borrow from.

16

WHY HOMES ARE REPOSSESSED

Lenders are willing to make home mortgage loans for fairly large amounts and at fairly low rates of interest because a valuable piece of property makes good collateral. When you get a loan to buy a home, you sign two important documents. The first—the note—describes your obligation to repay the loan each month. The second—the mortgage contract—gives the lender certain legal rights to the home in case you fail to fulfill your obligation to repay the loan. Without the home as collateral securing the loan, no lender would consider giving you such a large loan.

Of course, not everyone who signs a mortgage contract is able to live up to the financial obligation. Loss of a job, a major financial loss, or an unexpected burden could render a borrower insolvent and unable to continue making payments. Most mortgage contracts allow a grace period of 10 to 15 days after a payment is due before a penalty is added to the payment, and the loan is soon considered delinquent. When payments are generally three or more months behind, the loan is considered in default and the borrower is notified of the consequences of not keeping up with the payments. Local lenders sometimes work with borrowers who are having difficulty because of job loss or some other hardship, especially when it is obviously temporary. However, many loans are merely serviced by local lenders or specialized loan servicing companies, having been bought by a national institutional investor. These investors apply general policies to all loans and do not allow the local servicer to deviate from policy. After default, a lender's next step is to accelerate the loan (declare the full amount to be due immediately, not just the missed payments) and start foreclosure proceedings.

A loan can be in default and subject to foreclosure for any breach of the mortgage contract. For example, failing to insure a property adequately is a default of the mortgage contract. However, almost all foreclosures are the result of not making loan payments on time.

Although financial difficulty usually is at the root of delinquent payments, a homeowner who is unable to make payments could often sell the house and pay off the loan. However, if market conditions are not right, the borrower may not be able to sell the home for enough to cover the mortgage balance and the expenses of a sale. That is why home foreclosures are so frequent when local economies go into recession. Not only are people thrown out of work and incomes decreased, but market values of homes fall. Under these conditions, homeowners have been known to simply mail their house keys to the lender in lieu of the monthly payment. Still, they may be liable for the difference between their debt and the eventual sales price at foreclosure, called a "deficiency judgment."

When a lender accelerates the loan, the borrower has a certain amount of time to respond to this mandate. Foreclosure is the process by which the lender turns to the collateral property to satisfy the outstanding debt. The procedures used and the rights available to the borrower are established by state law and may differ markedly from state to state. The next several Keys describe various steps in the process in general terms. For your particular state, you will need to consult an attorney familiar with local law.

Author's note: Keys 17 through 22 provide information about foreclosures that may be helpful in understanding the process, but is not essential to the potential home buyer. The home buyer needs assurance from a qualified attorney or title company as to the quality of title being received, and any risks assumed. The home buyer must not assume those risks nor rely on information provided here as sufficient to avoid legal difficulties with acquisitions.

17

JUDICIAL FORECLOSURE

Rights of mortgage lenders and borrowers have evolved over time. The basic premise is to allow the lender to protect its investment in the event that the borrower fails to live up to the mortgage agreement. At the same time, the law aims to protect the borrower from a lender who wants to wrest away the mortgaged property wrongfully. We all have in mind a picture of the unscrupulous lender pouncing on a helpless borrower by claiming valuable property at the first sign of economic trouble. However, most lenders are more comfortable making loans than managing property and would prefer their borrowers to simply keep their loans current. When it becomes evident that the borrower is unable or unwilling to honor the obligation, all any lender wants to do is salvage whatever amount is possible from the collateral.

Foreclosure law is formed and enforced at the state level. For that reason, specific approaches to the problem of allocating rights between lender and borrower vary in each state. However, states fall into one of two categories of legal philosophy. The majority of the states subscribe to the idea that a mortgage establishes a special interest in the property as a lien. In the event of a default on the mortgage obligation, the lender may exercise a claim on the property that is satisfied in court proceedings. Other states provide the lender with rights similar to those of an owner of the property. In these states, the law establishes procedures for the sale of the property in the case of default. In general, lenders in these states are in a stronger position to protect their

46

interests than those in states following the lien philosophy. As a practical matter, the procedures of foreclosure and sale of the property have a similar effect in all states.

At one time, a borrower who was delinquent on a loan payment would have to forfeit all rights to the property, which became the property of the lender. This "strict foreclosure" has been phased out in many states in favor of law that provides the borrower a specified "equity of redemption." This means that the borrower has the right to redeem the property by satisfying the debt. When a lender forecloses a loan, it is this equity of redemption that is being foreclosed, or eliminated. All states provide borrowers with some period of time during which the borrower can avoid losing the property by paying off the loan, but the length of this period varies.

A lender who wants to foreclose petitions the court to cut off this period. In most cases, the borrower is allowed to occupy the property and may even sell it during this period. In some states, the mortgage contract provides that the lender can put the property up for sale in the event of a default; in others, the sale must be conducted under the sanction of the court. This latter procedure is referred to as "judicial foreclosure." It is a relatively time consuming and expensive process that virtually guarantees that the lender will be unable to fully satisfy the debt through sale proceeds. However, the purchaser of the property at the foreclosure sale, usually the lender, is assured of receiving a property free and clear of all encumbrances.

Lenders typically acquire the property at foreclosure although they would prefer a sale. Lenders can simply present their lien to acquire the property. Another party could bid more than the unpaid debt, taking the property away from the lender. However, the lender cannot profit from the foreclosure sale. Any excess over the sum of the unpaid debt plus back interest and foreclosure costs goes to the former owner.

18

NONJUDICIAL FORECLOSURE

In many states, the customary mortgage contract is worded to allow the lender to sell the property in the case of foreclosure without going through an extended court process. Such "power of sale" mortgages make it easier for the lender to recover the debt. Though the rights of the owner are not fully protected by the courts, these "nonjudicial" foreclosures are commonly used where state law allows.

In some states (Arizona, California, Colorado, Mississippi, Missouri, Tennessee, Texas, Oregon, Virginia, West Virginia, and the District of Columbia), the predominant type of mortgage used is the deed of trust. This mortgage provides for a trustee who is granted the power to sell the property in the event of default and foreclosure. The trustee must conduct the sale under strict guidelines established in the law of the state. However, the process is straightforward and is more predictable than the alternative of a court-monitored sale. (The disadvantage of not involving the courts is that it may leave the action open to later challenge and scrutiny by the courts. This is rarely the case, however, when the rules are clear and are followed strictly.)

The trustee must provide public notice of the sale. In most jurisdictions there is a certain time and place for the sale, most often the county courthouse on a designated day each month. If you are interested in participating, check periodically with the county clerk for notices of impending sales. Courthouses will have a bulletin board where notice of each property to be foreclosed is posted for several weeks before the sale. However, the notice may provide only a legal description that is adequate to locate the property on a survey map, and not describe its size, features, or condition. You have no right to visit private property just because it has been posted for foreclosure. However, the owners may invite you to visit if your intention is to purchase from them.

Foreclosure destroys all mortgage liens established after the time of the mortgage being foreclosed. Therefore, the buyer receives the property free and clear of the subject mortgage, as well as any mortgages that may have been added later. However, any claims established before the first mortgage was created are still in effect. It is important to have the title searched and to gain the protection provided by title insurance, especially when purchasing foreclosed property.

States where nonjudicial foreclosure sales are typically used include: Arizona, Alabama, Alaska, Georgia, Idaho, Maryland, Massachusetts, Minnesota, New Hampshire, New York, Rhode Island, South Dakota, and Wyoming. Also included are those states where the deed of trust is the predominant mortgage instrument (listed earlier).

19

DEED IN LIEU OF FORECLOSURE

All defaults need not result in foreclosure sales. In some cases, a borrower faced with foreclosure may be able to sell the property prior to losing it. The new owner may be able to assume the old mortgage and bring it up to date. More often, the buyer will arrange new financing and retire the old loan. A distressed owner may have an incentive to sell even though the price is below the mortgage balance owed, since a foreclosure may destroy his or her ability to get another mortgage loan. In many cases, however, the owner cannot afford or is unwilling to sell a home for less than what is owed.

Some borrowers are under the impression that they can merely turn ownership over to the lender and thereby satisfy the debt. During economically depressed periods, it is not uncommon for homeowners to mail in the keys to their homes instead of making up the mortgage payments. However, a lender does not have to accept such a transfer in payment for the debt. There is a good chance that in the ensuing foreclosure sale, the property will not sell for enough to cover the debt plus expenses. In that case, the borrower may still be liable for a deficiency judgment for the difference.

On the other hand, sometimes lenders accept the transfer. Title to the property goes to the lender in a transaction termed "deed in lieu of foreclosure." When the lender accepts such a deed, the right to a deficiency judgment is waived. In these cases, the lender has determined that possessing the property without delay is preferable to the cost and risk of pursuing both a foreclosure proceeding and a deficiency judgment suit. Often, the borrower is "judgment proof," meaning that he or she has little wealth available to satisfy a judgment, even if successful in court.

What this means to the buyer seeking foreclosed property is that some homes may become part of a lender's inventory without going through a foreclosure sale. While you may not have the opportunity to bid at a foreclosure sale on these properties, you may be able to buy from the lender's inventory (see Keys 26–30). One thing you should recognize about such properties is that the deed in lieu of foreclosure process may not resolve all claims against the property. Therefore, when buying from the lender's inventory, it is important to receive a warranty deed to protect against future claims against the property.

20

FORECLOSURE SALES

The end result of a foreclosure proceeding is a sale of the property. Money from the sale goes to satisfy the outstanding debt plus accrued interest and expenses. If there is any money remaining, it is used to pay any junior lien holders on the property and, finally, the borrower. If, as often happens, the proceeds are not enough to cover the debt, a deficiency judgment may be brought against the borrower.

The foreclosure sale is conducted as an open auction where anyone interested in the property may enter a bid. Procedures for conducting a sale are set by the courts or within state law and vary from state to state. However, some features are universal. Adequate notice of the time and place of the sale, as well as a description of the property, must be given to both the borrower and the public. This may include an official notice at the county courthouse and some type of advertisement in the local legal newspaper. This is to insure that the public is notified of the sale and any interested party may bid. Procedures used for entering bids and accepting a winner are written in the law as well.

When a judicial foreclosure is used, the sale is conducted under the instructions and supervision of the courts. In some states, a minimum acceptable price will be set by the court. Some states regulate how much a lender can recover through foreclosure. In all cases, the court must accept the results of the sale before it is finalized. This requirement is to protect the borrower from a large deficiency judgment resulting from too low a sales price.

Nonjudicial foreclosure sales are conducted by the trustee or designated person in the mortgage contract.

Procedures are described in the contract and are consistent with state law. There is some potential that nonjudicial sales will be set aside because of a challenge from the borrower. However, most borrowers who feel aggrieved by the sales proceedings will sue for damages rather than set aside the sale. Therefore, as a practical matter, nonjudicial sales are as safe for the successful bidder as are judicial sales.

In almost all foreclosure sales, the lender is the successful bidder on the property. A lender may bid a specific dollar amount or simply present the debt owed as the bid amount. Outside bidders are encouraged to bid so that the sale is more fair and less likely to be challenged. The winning bidder receives the property in the same legal condition the property was in prior to making the mortgage. The foreclosed mortgage and any junior mortgages made afterwards are eliminated. However, the title may still be clouded by any right of redemption provided to the borrower by state law. This can be a serious drawback to bidders in states that provide a lengthy right of redemption.

An individual investor may feel intimidated bidding against institutions at a foreclosure sale. Most lenders, however, will be pleased to see the property go to an outside party, alleviating them of receiving the property and reselling it. Their primary objective will be to assure that the winning bid is not too low and that they do not receive what is owed on the mortgage. If you feel confident that the property can be obtained at a good price, bid. You may find it more advantageous, however, to buy from the lender after the foreclosure sale is consummated.

21

QUALITY OF THE TITLE RECEIVED AT FORECLOSURE SALES

One reason for hesitation about buying at a foreclosure sale is concern over title to the property. Depending on how the sale is conducted and on state law, the buyer may have a perfectly good deed or may face the possibility of losing the property in a legal dispute. You should check carefully with an attorney and title company, and not buy if there is any doubt of good title.

First of all, recall that foreclosure by the mortgage holder effectively cuts off the rights of the borrower to the property and eliminates the mortgage lien. It also eliminates any subordinate mortgages or liens created after the subject mortgage (except for tax liens held by local government and vendors liens that may be held by anyone who worked on the property without being paid in full). If you purchase the property at the foreclosure sale, you obtain the same rights enjoyed by the borrower before the loan was made.

There are several potential limitations to these rights, however. First, you will probably receive a special warranty deed at the sale. This type of deed guarantees that any claims to the property that were created while the seller owned it have been cleared. However, it makes no promises about claims arising before the property was foreclosed. Be wary of a quitclaim deed, as it provides no guarantee. In such a deed the grantor gives up whatever rights he or she has, but may not actually have any ownership rights at all.

Second, if the property was not foreclosed under the supervision of the courts, there is a chance that the sale will be challenged and thrown out. This could result from failure to follow the procedures provided in the law or because the winning bid is considered not to be a fair price for the property. As mentioned in the previous Key, borrowers who challenge a sale generally seek damages rather than to nullify the sale, so the chances of losing the property are small. In any case, beware of a situation where the winning bid appears ridiculously low.

Anyone bidding at a foreclosure sale should determine that the foreclosed loan represented the only lien. Otherwise, other existing debts carry over to the new property owner.

From the time a mortgage is declared in default to the time it is foreclosed, the borrower has an equitable right of redemption. That means the borrower could prevent the foreclosure sale by paying back the loan plus accrued interest. Once the lender accelerates the loan, the option of merely bringing the payments up to date is lost. However, in many states, the borrower retains the right to redeem the property even after foreclosure and sale of the property. This is called the statutory right of redemption and can vary by state from zero to many months.

The possibility that the borrower could reclaim the property can be a nuisance to anyone who buys at the sale. While the chances of a previous owner actually redeeming the property are remote, you may have concerns about spending for renovation, repair, and remodeling of the structure. Before bidding at a foreclosure sale, know what kind of right of redemption is provided borrowers in your state. If it is a lengthy period, you may want to avoid foreclosure sales and focus your efforts on properties that have been acquired by lenders, their "Real Estate Owned" (REO) inventory.

22

AFTER THE FORECLOSURE SALE

In most states, the lender is allowed to bid on the property at the foreclosure sale. In fact, the lender is often the only serious bidder and ends up with the property. The lender presents the mortgage debt as a bid on the property and obtains it with no additional cash expense. Other bidders must come up with cash or arrange financing for the price of the property. In addition, questions about the quality of the title may discourage outside bidders. In states that provide a lengthy right of redemption, the possibility of the property reverting to a previous owner is an additional deterrent.

The courts recognize the possibility that a foreclosure sale may not yield a fair price and often attempt to set a minimum price for the property. A price that is too low will make the borrower liable for an unfairly large deficiency judgment. For example, in some states a lender must be prepared to show that the highest bid is a reasonable percentage of the property's market value. This raises the possibility that the sale will be inconclusive if no one is willing to bid the minimum. In most cases, the lender wishes to avoid an inconclusive sale (as well as ward off challenge suits by the borrower) and may offer the minimum to acquire the property.

In today's complex residential financial market, the present lender is not always the entity that originally made the loan. Many home loans are originated (first made) by mortgage banking companies and mortgage brokers. Mortgage bankers package the loans they originate and sell them on what is called the "secondary" mortgage market. This market has grown rapidly in recent years especially by accommodating lending institutions that kept the loans they originated. The secondary mortgage market (not to be confused with second mortgages) handles trading for the majority of first mortgages, as these are often traded within a few days after origination. Although the mortgage originator continues to service the loan (collect payments and maintain the escrow account) the loan is actually owned by someone else. This may be a private investor that buys loans. In most cases, the loan is one in a large pool of loans held by a specialized secondary market entity. The largest of these entities were created by the federal government, but are privately owned. The Federal National Mortgage Association, or Fannie Mae, holds most of its loans in a large portfolio. The Federal Home Loan Mortgage Corporation, or Freddie Mac, sells portions of its portfolio to investors. Each of these organizations, but especially Fannie Mae, may be the initiator and winning bidder at a foreclosure sale on loans it holds.

You may have heard of Ginnie Mae, nickname for the Government National Mortgage Association (GNMA), though its role in foreclosures is minimal. Ginnie Mae is a government agency that subsidizes loans made to qualified low income homeowners.

Loans that are insured or guaranteed involve additional entities when they are foreclosed. When a loan is guaranteed by the Federal Housing Administration (FHA) or a private mortgage insurance company, the lender has a claim against the insurer when the borrower defaults. The insurer may pay off the amount of the claim and leave the lender to foreclose. However, often the insurer finds it better to acquire the property and try to recoup losses through resale. The Veterans Administration (VA), which guarantees loans for qualified veterans, may either pay off the amount of the guarantee or acquire the property. When the property is foreclosed they may offer a "no-bid," meaning that they pay their guarantee to the mortgage lender, usually serviced by a mortgage banker. That can load up a mortgage banker with unwanted property that may be sold as a forced sale.

Savings and loan (S&L) associations and commercial banks (CB) are covered by insurance that protects depositors in the event of insolvency by the institution. In many cases, the Federal Deposit Insurance Corporation (FDIC), which is the government agency providing the insurance, acquires the assets of the failing bank, including properties previously repossessed by the institution and non-performing loans on properties that will soon be foreclosed.

When lenders, companies, and government organizations acquire properties, they place them in special inventories. For lending institutions, this inventory is called "real estate owned" (REO) or "other real estate owned" (OREO). These terms refer to real estate the bank owns other than the property it needs to conduct its banking business.

These organizations attempt to manage the properties to produce whatever income possible, but their intent is to sell them off as expeditiously as possible. They may advertise and take bids, list with professional brokers, or hold auctions. These inventories are the richest source of potential bargain properties available. However, each organization has its own operating procedures and the prospective buyer must be familiar with them. (The procedures of the major holders of REO are described in Key 26.)

23

BIDDING AND FINANCING OVERVIEW FOR A REPOSSESSED HOME

There are various methods used to accept bids and select winners. This Key serves to explain some of the terms used to describe those methods and the financing needed in order to buy a repossessed home.

A **sealed bid** process requires bidders to submit offers with no knowledge of competing bids. There may or may not be an asking price for the property (in some cases, an acceptable bid must be at or near the asking price). The bid should cover the entire transaction, including any requirement for seller payment of closing costs or seller-provided financing. Usually, such bids are collected over a short period when a listing is first released. This allows adequate time for all interested bidders to respond.

When the bids are opened, they are arranged in order of highest value. If there is a minimum bid price, any bids below the standard are eliminated. If the top bids are identical, the agency will select the winner on the basis of a set of priorities. Generally, cash bids are preferred to ones calling for financing. In some cases, there is a target group (such as someone who will occupy the home) that will receive favorable treatment.

The winning bidder is informed of the results of the selection process and given time to respond. Those who made unsuccessful bids receive their deposits back. A winning bidder who does not respond, will, in most cases, forfeit the deposit, though there are provisions for hardship cases. Procedures for choosing another bid vary. If the winner goes through with the purchase, the deposit is applied to the price.

Open bidding works much like any real estate transaction. The prospective buyer makes an initial offer in response to the seller's announcement of the availability of the property. The seller may accept the offer, reject the offer (cutting off negotiations), or respond with a counter-offer. The counter rejects the terms of the buyer's offer and suggests a new amount. A series of counter-offers from each side may continue until both sides agree or one party cuts off the negotiation. When an agreement is settled, the final contract of sale is signed and a closing date set.

Before placing a bid for property, obtain as much information as is available about the bidding process and any procedures for inspecting the property. Note, particularly, any restrictions placed on bids and any reservations or priorities set for who can bid. In many cases, bids may be placed through a real estate agent approved by the selling agency. Finally, try to ascertain when the agency will announce the winning bid. You may find it not worthwhile if your bid is tied up in indecision for an extended period.

Financing. Most purchases of real estate require some type of financing. The mortgage lending industry in this country is well developed and is flexible enough to accommodate most borrowers' needs. However, needing a mortgage loan to buy repossessed property can be a problem.

A mortgage loan is secured by the real property purchased with the proceeds. In other words, the lender looks to the value of the property as protection in case the borrower defaults on the loan. That is why the lender requires a property description (survey) and appraisal of the property before approving the loan.

In many situations, if you buy repossessed property you need to have pre-arranged financing. That is because many sellers do not allow contingencies in the sales contract that would allow buyers to apply for a mortgage loan after the contract is signed. Such a contingency allows you to back out of the agreement and recover your earnest money deposit if the loan is not approved (in fact, most contingencies state the terms of the loan that must be obtained). If you know before bidding that financing will be approved, you can pursue the property with some assurance that a transaction will result and that your deposit will not be lost.

While a lender will not approve a loan without the collateral specified, it may be possible to get pre-approved based on your financial position. The lender may run a credit check, verify your income and other financial resources, and specify the limit of your borrowing ability. You may even obtain a general description of the quality of property that could be financed through that institution. The lender may rule out condominiums or duplexes, for example. If you need FHA financing, you will want to know any restrictions that apply to the property to be financed. You will have the additional advantage of knowing how big a loan is possible, so you will know the most you can bid for a property.

Another option is to use your present home or some other property you currently own to secure the loan. This option offers the advantage of completely pre-arranged financing with no risk that the loan on new property will be turned down after you have committed to buy the property. The disadvantage is that you are putting additional property at risk should you be forced to default on the loan. Also, you need to have substantial equity built up in the properties to be able to mortgage them. This type of financing can be expensive, especially if the property already has a mortgage on it.

Seller-provided financing can be an advantage, even when the terms are similar to those available in the market.

The financing goes with the sale and, therefore, you won't lose the transaction because financing cannot be arranged. Of course, most sellers who are willing to finance would really prefer cash. So if you are depending on seller financing, you are at a competitive disadvantage to cash bidders.

24

FINDING FORECLOSED HOMES

An investor has three opportunities to purchase a property that has been or is in danger of foreclosure. The first occurs when a homeowner defaults on a mortgage loan and the lender takes action to begin the foreclosure process. A legal notice, referred to as "lis pendens," is filed in the public record (a notice of default is recorded for nonjudicial foreclosure). Therefore, an investor interested in buying homes in pre-foreclosure may monitor the courthouse records for these notices.

The second opportunity comes at the end of the foreclosure process. If the lender uses judicial foreclosure to recover the debt (determined by the mortgage contract and state law), the property will be auctioned to the highest bidder on the courthouse steps. Although the lender ends up the buyer in the vast majority of cases, anyone may tender a bid at the sale. If the investor submits the winning bid, the property is hers. Public notice is required several weeks prior to the sale, so that bidders may have time to investigate the property. These notices will be posted at a set place within the courthouse and may be advertised in the local newspapers, as well.

Finally, investors can buy properties that have been repossessed by lenders, mortgage investors, and insurers. There is no official public notice when these properties become available, but the selling organizations take it upon themselves to publicize their availability. Some sellers publish lists and booklets of properties and maintain searchable listings on the Internet. Some establish offices or divisions to market the properties. Many sign listing contracts with local real estate agents. A few closely guard their list and make it available only to customers or stockholders.

The point is that the process of finding properties varies depending on which stage of foreclosure you prefer. However, in each case, finding properties requires knowledge of the system and the time and effort to monitor the various notification systems.

Where there is a need to organize information, there is a profit opportunity for those doing the organizing. After all, why should each investor track down this data, when someone could do it once for all of them? Consequently, there are services that monitor *lis pendens* and foreclosure sale notices and collect listings of Real Estate Owned (REO) inventories and make them available to paying customers.

The first such services were a by-product of the record searches conducted by title insurance companies. Although the courthouse records are public information and access is free of charge, finding useful information can be extremely time consuming, as well as confusing for someone without a legal background. Therefore, a service that makes this data more accessible has significant value.

The advent of the Internet makes these services even more valuable. There are a great number of foreclosure information services with Internet presence, as any Web browser search will verify. The following is a briefing of what you might find:

- Some are national in scope, but most are regional or even restricted to one metropolitan area. The local should be okay if you consider buying only in one area.
- Most include some nonresidential property and undeveloped land along with homes. These can be a good source of income properties.
- The actual listings come in several forms. Some sell annual or monthly printed catalogs that can be

ordered over the Internet. Others maintain on-line databases that can be searched by location and property type that can be accessed by subscribers for an annual or monthly fee. Many of these offer a trial search or temporary complimentary subscription. One service allows you to do a limited search to see if there are any properties in your area. If you find properties, you can get more information by subscribing.

- The bulk of the information concerns REO properties held by lending institutions and government agencies. There usually is a brief description, perhaps an address, and who to contact if you wish to inspect the property and place a bid. Many also monitor notices of default and foreclosure for those who wish to pursue a pre-foreclosure purchase or bid at foreclosure sales.
- Some sell books and newsletters that provide news and how-to information on foreclosure investing. Many provide a good deal of this type of information for free on their Web site. A particularly informative one is the Real Estate Library located at *http://therealestatelibrary.com*. Also available are chat groups where investors can exchange information among themselves.

The level of quality varies considerably among the services available. Many of these appear to be very useful for the active investor or even someone looking for a good deal on a home. Unfortunately, some may offer little more than can be found on one's own. Fortunately, in many cases, the costs of trying a service is not high ($30–$40 for a monthly report or one month's subscription). Several provide descriptive information about what is available without requiring payment. For most investors, a bit of investigative work and modest investment is probably warranted. If you are looking to make a one-time purchase of a home for your own use, you might skip these services and contact your local HUD or

VA office for a list of homes or authorized real estate agents in your area. (Check out the HUD Web site, *http://www.hud.gov*, for access to HUD homes as well as linkages to other government and quasi-government sellers of repossessed homes.) There is no charge for this information.

25

WORKING UP A BID

There are various procedures by which you can make an offer on repossessed property. One method popular with governmental agencies is the sealed bid, whereby you submit an offer with the terms kept secret from other bidders. You bid at an auction, too, but then you know what others are bidding. Quite a bit of inventory can be bid on by making an offer through an agent and negotiating a contract just like any other piece of real estate.

The key to making an offer, regardless of the method, is setting a reservation price and sticking to it. A reservation price is the highest price you will pay for a property without paying more than it is worth to you. If market conditions are in your favor, you should be able to get the property for something less than your reservation price. Your first offer can be for much less than your maximum. The gap between this initial offer and the reservation price provides room to negotiate, if necessary.

Your reservation price is not necessarily market value. There may be features of the property that are especially valuable to you, or some that have no value. Therefore, everyone's maximum value is different. In a competitive bidding process, the winner will be the one who values the property highest. It is tempting to pursue a property when bidding starts. Remember, however, that unless the property is priceless to you, winning the bid at too high a price nullifies the whole point of buying repossessed property. After all, you are in this market to obtain a bargain.

To set your reservation price, you must know something about what is available in the current market and, preferably, what sold and for how much. Since you are an active buyer, this should not be too difficult. You may have information on asking prices (maybe even some sales data) for properties that are very similar to the one you are considering buying. Note any differences in the properties that would affect their value to you. If the subject has some important feature that is lacking in the comparison property (appraisers call these "comparables"), add an amount to the asking price. If the subject is deficient in some feature, subtract an amount. How much to add or subtract? If the feature is something that could be added, adjust by the cost of making the addition. If not, you must judge how much you would be willing to pay to have the feature. Ignore items that you would not care about (or, if you will rent out the home, items that would not add to the rent you could charge).

Once you have a reservation price, you can devise a bidding strategy. If the procedure is sealed bid with no minimum limit on bid amounts, deduct about 10 percent from your reservation price and submit the amount. The amount of discount depends on how popular you think the property will be. If you have lost several bids previously on similar properties, you might bid your full reservation price. If the seller has set a minimum bid amount, compare it to your reservation price. If it is too high, you might pass and wait for the property to come down in price. In an auction, your reservation price tells you when to stop bidding. Opening bids are usually mandated by the auctioneer.

In a normal negotiation between seller and buyer, you will go through several states of offer and counter-offer. You can offer something substantially lower than your reservation price as an initial offer. Negotiations can continue until the seller agrees to your price or you reach your reservation limit.

If you are seeking seller financing, the terms of the loan should be factored into your maximum price. This can be done by calculating the monthly payments you would pay with market financing at your reservation price. This becomes the maximum monthly cost you would be willing to bear to obtain the property.

26

BUYING FROM LENDING INSTITUTIONS

Savings and loan associations, commercial banks, and even some credit unions make home mortgage loans. Today, many of these loans are sold into the secondary market. However, a sizable proportion are held in portfolio by the lending institution. When defaults occur on these loans, the institution ends up obtaining the property in most instances. The properties are placed in an REO inventory to be managed and resold to the public.

The methods used to sell REO properties may vary with each institution. In fact, one institution may use a variety of methods over time, depending on the size of its inventory and what seems to be working at the time. Some may even consider access to its REO a privilege reserved for account holders.

If the inventory is relatively small, as it is under normal conditions, the institution will probably grant exclusive listings with local real estate brokers. An exclusive listing gives one broker the right to sell the property for a commission to the exclusion of all other brokers. This provides the security necessary to allow the broker to advertise the listing. Other brokers work with the listing broker, when the listing broker belongs to a multiple listing service.

When the inventory is unusually large, it may be worthwhile for the institution to establish an in-house management and sales staff. If a large number of properties are of the same type or are located in the same area, the institution may hold an auction.

Therefore, there are a number of ways to bid upon

REO property. You may go directly to lending institutions in your area and inquire about currently available homes. You may ask a local broker about homes being sold by lending institutions. (Recognize that a broker's responsibility is to the seller. Ethically, the broker should not disclose details about the seller's need to sell the property. However, the identity of the seller can be disclosed. In fact, brokers will often tell prospective buyers that the owner is an institution that would like to dispose of the property quickly.) Lastly, you may participate in auctions conducted by lending institutions.

In most cases, you will find that institutions act much like any other property sellers. There are government-mandated regulations on how they sell properties that can lead to advantages and disadvantages for the buyer.

Advantages. The institution will be relatively anxious to sell the home. The home is probably vacant and not producing any income for the lender. In addition, the lender may have remodeled and repaired the building to make it more presentable. The lender may be willing to make special financing available on the purchase. These factors work in favor of the buyer.

Disadvantages. The biggest disadvantage is that the lender may be slow to respond to offers from potential buyers. There may be some type of administrative committee that must approve sales, especially when the bid is below appraised value. This can be frustrating for the bidder. There also may be a minimum price the lender is determined to get. It may be that the lender is trying to avoid declaring a loss on the loan. A reservation price that is too high may stall the negotiations, although the lender may be able to counter the higher price with favorable financing terms.

The drawbacks do not rule out this avenue to bargain homes. Indeed, lending institution REO inventories are normally one of the best sources of repossessed homes. You will need to understand the ways in which the negotiation can stall and be prepared to offer ways around the problem.

27

BUYING A HUD HOME

The Federal Housing Administration (FHA) provides insurance against default on home mortgage loans. When covered by this insurance, a lender may provide a loan that supplies more than the standard 80 percent of the purchase price of a home. When defaults occur, the FHA often ends up with the home following the foreclo sure sale. Because the FHA provides insurance on low-down-payment loans, defaults are more common than on conventional loans. This means HUD usually has one of the larger inventories of repossessed homes.

Sometimes known as "HUD homes," these properties are offered for sale to the public (FHA is a division of the Department of Housing and Urban Development, or HUD). You may obtain a list of available homes from your local HUD sales office (see page 158) or go through a real estate broker. The agency does not in general use exclusive listings with brokers but will accept bids through brokers who are on an approved list. (HUD has an excellent Web site accessed through *http://www.hud.gov.* If you want to see homes available in your area, go to *http://www.hud.gov/homesale.html.*)

Occasionally, HUD will place advertisements in the classified section of local newspapers. (Don't be confused with the reference to HUD rather than the FHA. Whereas the FHA handles the insurance program, HUD is the parent agency that markets and sells the properties.)

Most homes will be offered with an asking price stated. Since there is a limit on the amount of loan that can be covered by FHA insurance, the homes held by HUD will be somewhat modest relative to the market. Homes may include condominiums and even some multi-family buildings. The agency generally does not repair or remodel the properties, except in cases of dangerous situations. If a home is in good enough condition to satisfy FHA standards, a purchase loan on the property may be eligible for insurance coverage. Some homes may include a bonus for fix-up expenses. The FHA does not make loans directly and, therefore, does not finance the properties it sells.

Once you have inspected the property and decided on an offering price, you may submit a sealed bid to HUD. General procedure calls for holding all bids for the full offer period. When the bids are opened, the highest net offer is accepted. Bidders who will occupy the home are given priority, after which bids from investors are considered.

A bid should state the offering price and any special costs to be incurred by HUD. The agency will pay some of the buyer's closing costs and any brokerage commission on the sale. However, these costs are deducted from the bid price for the purpose of determining the highest net bid to HUD. For example, someone offering $30,000 with no cost to HUD would beat out a bid of $31,000 calling for HUD to pay a commission of $1,500.

The bidding process is straightforward. On the other hand, properties must be examined carefully, for they may be in poor condition. Don't expect a luxury home in the inventory, but you may find some good income property. Finally, HUD provides no financing but the FHA may provide insurance on a loan you arrange with a lending institution or mortgage banker.

28

BUYING FROM THE VETERANS ADMINISTRATION

The Veterans Administration (VA) guarantees home loans for eligible military veterans. When a veteran defaults on the loan, the VA often buys the home in lieu of paying out the amount of the guarantee. When mortgage foreclosures have been frequent in an area, the VA is a good source of foreclosed homes. (Addresses of VA Regional Offices are provided in the Appendix.)

The VA markets homes in a similar fashion to HUD (see Key 27). Bids are accepted from the public (they may be entered through a real estate broker or directly), properties are offered in "as is" condition, bids must be submitted without contingencies, and a five- to ten-day waiting period is used to collect bids. However, there are some important differences.

The VA does not give brokers exclusive contracts to list properties, but it does designate a managing broker to coordinate sales of properties in an area. You may go directly to this broker or work through a broker of your choice. Unlike the FHA, the VA does not deduct the broker's commission from the bid price. However, you must offer the list price for a property unless it is designated for a negotiated price.

Another important distinction is that the VA will finance the homes it sells. These loans are fixed-rate loans at the current VA ceiling interest rate. Down payment requirements are low, in many cases as low as 5 percent of the price. Furthermore, you do not have to be an eligible veteran to qualify for this financing.

If you have cash or have arranged financing elsewhere, the VA offers discounts for cash bids. Recently, these discounts were as much as 10 percent of the list price. In addition, the VA will pay some of the closing costs for cash bids (this usually consists of paying all or some of the discount points on a loan from a third party). Finally, cash offers are approved more quickly than those calling for seller financing.

Homes held by the VA may be comparable in quality and size to those owned by the FHA. The primary advantage of buying from the VA is the possibility of getting favorable financing with a low down payment. The trade-off is that you may have to bid list price for the home.

Brokers will have a special form on which to submit an offer for a VA-home. Preferential treatment is accorded those who will occupy the residence as a home (but investors may also bid), and those who make larger down payments may receive a lower interest rate. Discovering how much the previous owner owed upon default is irrelevant. Once the VA forecloses, a new ball game begins, based on the appraised value of the home the VA gets, as provided by a real estate appraiser.

29

BUYING FROM FANNIE OR FREDDIE

Fannie Mae and Freddie Mac are not government agencies, but are related to the federal government. Moreover, both organizations acquire homes through repossession and offer them to the public.

The Federal National Mortgage Association (FNMA), also referred to as Fannie Mae, was created by the federal government to help organize a secondary market in mortgage loans. This means FNMA buys loans that have been originated by others: mortgage bankers, banks and savings and loan associations. FNMA loans may be kept as investments or sold to investors in "pools." FNMA is a private organization owned by stockholders (though the U.S. government appoints some members to its board of directors). For the most part, FNMA operates as a private business.

Because FNMA owns loans, it often obtains properties when the loans are foreclosed. Like other owners of repossessed homes, the agency markets these properties to the public. The homes in inventory vary in value and quality. There is a limit to the amount of loan FNMA can acquire, but it is much larger than the limit on FHA loans. This means that FNMA will probably have some higher priced homes than the FHA. Mortgage limits are changed with the type of loan and geographic location, and are also changed over time.

Most of the homes in the FNMA inventory are less than five years old. When necessary, the agency will remodel or repair the homes to make them more salable. However, some are offered "as is."

The agency uses a variety of methods to sell homes. It contracts with local brokers to list properties. It may advertise homes in the local paper. Occasionally, auctions are held on a group of homes in an area. (You may obtain a list of available homes in your area by accessing their Web site at *http://www.fanniemae.com/homes/index.html*.)

An asking price is set for all properties based on a professional appraisal and an opinion of probable selling price from a local broker. However, the agency is willing to negotiate a price with an interested buyer. In addition, the agency is willing to offer financing when necessary to complete a sale.

There are several advantages to working with FNMA. The agency is relatively free from bureaucratic requirements that slow down negotiations and final approval. It is fairly easy to get information and place a bid. Prices are negotiable and financing is available.

FNMA has less of a social welfare goal than does HUD. Consequently, investors are welcome to bid competitively with potential occupants. Investors may find themselves at a disadvantage in securing as much financing as owner-occupants.

The Federal Home Loan Mortgage Corporation (FHLMC), also known as Freddie Mac, is very similar to Fannie Mae in organization and operation. Freddie Mac offers its homes ready for occupancy, with 5 percent down financing, and no mortgage insurance premiums. (To find a home, check the special Web site established for this purpose: *http://www.homesteps.com/*. You may register on the Web to have information sent to you when homes become available in your area.)

30

OTHER SOURCES OF FORECLOSED PROPERTY

Private Mortgage Insurance Companies. In general, before a lender will make a low-down-payment loan, the loan must either be guaranteed by the VA or Farmers Home Administration (FmHA) or be covered by private mortgage (default) insurance. Before the FHA began offering such insurance, there were private companies that served this role. During the housing boom following World War II, private mortgage insurers were relatively inactive compared to the FHA. In recent years, the companies have regained presence in the market, mainly because of the limits placed on the size of loan FHA can insure.

Private mortgage insurance works much like FHA insurance. The main difference is that private insurance covers losses up to only 20 percent of the loan, whereas the FHA generally stands behind the entire loan amount. When a borrower on a loan covered by private insurance defaults, the lender forecloses and takes title at the foreclosure sale. The lender then files a claim with the insurance company for a portion of total losses incurred. The insurance company has the choice of taking title to the property by paying the entire loan or reimbursing the lender by the amount of the claim and letting the lender keep the property.

Because of their limited exposure to loss, private insurers do not take title to as many properties as does the FHA or VA. Nevertheless, these companies may be worth investigating, particularly if there is a headquarters in your area. The oldest, and largest, is the Mortgage Guaranty Insurance Corporation (MGIC). These insurance companies may use a variety of marketing methods and have no rigid procedures for entertaining bids. You may contact the company directly for information, particularly if there have been a large number of foreclosures in the area lately, or look for ads in the paper. Many properties are higher in quality and price than those held by the FHA and VA.

Private mortgage insurers are motivated sellers who know that they lose money by holding vacant property. They have less administrative red tape than government agencies and fewer properties to monitor. Consequently, they may be much easier to deal with and may have property that appeals to your tastes. However, their inventory will be much smaller than that of government agencies.

There is a popular misconception that mortgage insurance serves to protect the life of the borrower. The kind of mortgage insurance referred to here is default insurance, which has nothing to do with life insurance. As the term implies, default insurance is used to insure the lender in the event of a default. The borrower pays the cost, generally when the down payment is under 20 percent. Mortgage default insurance costs vary with the down payment. For a typical 10 percent down payment, the cost is 2 percent of the full amount borrowed at closing, and an annual charge of ¼ of 1 percent of the loan, in addition to all interest and principal payments.

Life insurance to the extent of the loan amount is often available to home owners, and may also be called mortgage insurance, though it is more precisely called mortgage life insurance. Its purpose is to pay off the loan if the bread-winner dies, so the surviving family household members can live debt-free. Often, term insurance is available at a lower cost and will provide the same protection. Nevertheless, the type of mortgage insurance company referred to in this Key offers mortgage default insurance, not life insurance.

The Federal Deposit Insurance Corporation (FDIC) is a government agency created to insure deposit accounts at commercial banks. You probably have seen signs at your local bank advertising this coverage. When a bank fails, the FDIC moves in and either arranges a merger with a healthy bank or closes down the institution and takes over the bank. In either case, the FDIC obtains the assets of the failed institution (in merger cases, the FDIC may take assets the merging bank does not want). These assets include any REO held by the bank.

At one time, the Federal Savings and Loan Insurance Corporation (FSLIC) was the insurer for savings and loan associations. When FSLIC became insolvent in the late 1980s, its responsibilities were transferred to the FDIC.

The FDIC generally markets properties through exclusive listings with local brokers. In addition, regional offices have sales staffs that will receive sealed bids for properties. From time to time, there may be auctions when enough properties exist to make one feasible. Prices and terms are negotiable. The FDIC can provide seller financing, if necessary. These interim loans have terms of three to five years with a long-term amortization schedule and a balloon payment requirement. For more information, see your broker or the closest sales office of FDIC. It will be listed in your phone directory under "Federal Deposit Insurance Corporation." Some directories print government agencies on colored paper in the front or rear of the book. If there is no listing in your local directory, try the nearest major city.

As the FDIC's inventory diminishes, there may be a policy change that will shift their inventory to another agency, or a plan to dispose of it themselves more quickly. Such a change could create brief but excellent opportunities for bargain hunters. Stay in touch with real estate publications and people in the real estate market to be informed of possible changes, not only for a change in FDIC policy, but for any matter.

Relocation Companies. Homes held by relocation companies are not foreclosed homes, but offer opportunities to negotiate good bargains with highly motivated sellers. Furthermore, the fact that a relocation company is trying to sell a home, rather than its resident-owner, usually means that a buyers' market exists, and good prices should result.

Companies with offices or other facilities around the country periodically need to transfer employees from one location to another. This is particularly true of executive and technical personnel. Often these employees buy homes, even though they are aware of the possibilities of frequent relocation. When market conditions are good, selling these homes is no problem and often is an additional source of income for the homeowner. However, in slow markets, an employee may not be able to sell quickly without taking a sizable loss. Many companies assist employees by reimbursing losses or buying the home from the employee. There are firms that specialize in marketing these homes and they are often referred to as relocation companies.

When a relocation company takes over a home, it will usually refurbish the property, if needed, to make it more appealing to buyers. This generally means a new carpet and coat of paint. The property is put back on the market by listing it with a broker. Therefore, the way to find such homes is by contacting a broker who is a member of the local Multiple Listing Service (the MLS is a system that allows any member broker to sell any home in the system). Brokers frequently hang a "relocation company" sign on the "for sale" sign to make the buyer's motivation obvious to the market. It will also signal a message that the house is ready to be moved into, so there need not be any negotiation on the date of possession.

In most aspects, buying a home from a relocation company is just like buying from any other seller. However, the company may be more flexible, since the home is vacant and is costing the company money to hold. In most cases, the company should be amenable to reasonable offers. Do not expect to bargain for seller financing. On the other hand, the company may be willing to pay some closing costs. In addition, you will be able to include contingencies in the contract for financing, inspections, and other considerations. This is usually not possible when bidding on foreclosed homes.

Don't expect to buy one of these homes at a rock bottom price. In most cases, these are quality homes and should command decent prices in all but completely devastated markets. Do expect to find a motivated seller who will work with you to try to reach an agreement.

31

SELLER DISCLOSURE AND THE MEANING OF "AS IS"

In most housing transactions you have some recourse to the seller for failing to disclose certain defects. Often this is not meaningful because sellers move away and are difficult to reach or have so few assets that it is not worthwhile to pursue them. Still, if a seller or a broker has failed to disclose a defect or lied about it, you may be able to hold the individual responsible—unless that person sold the house "as is."

In many states, there are disclosure requirements for structural defects, termite infestation, lead-based paint, underground storage tanks, asbestos, and other conditions. A seller is obligated to inform you of these known hazards. If the property is offered "as is," however, you accept it in its present condition, whatever that may be. The words "as is" should set off an alarm that something may be wrong. Be certain to have a professional inspector check out the problem very carefully (but be aware that the standard inspection performed before closing covers only *visible* defects; an inspector generally is not responsible for structural problems that are covered by wallboard, carpet or other components of the house).

The "as is" clause may not protect the seller from failure to disclose latent or hidden defects. For example, suppose there had been a serious fire, the damage from which was completely concealed. The buyer could not detect such on inspection, so the "as is" provision might not protect the seller because the defect was hidden. A seller must disclose this even when selling "as is." You should know that this disclosure requirement does not apply when buying property from a lending institution. Unless some type of warranty is explicitly provided, you should not assume the property is in habitable condition until thoroughly inspected.

It is generally a good idea to perform your inspections well in advance of closing, whether or not the property is offered "as is." When it is sold "as is," be especially wary of its condition. Include in your purchase contract a statement giving you the right to various inspections, with enough time to perform them, such as ten business days after the acceptance of the sales or purchase contract, whatever the agreement is called.

How about "stigmatized" properties? These are homes where some gruesome crime was committed, a well-known suicide occurred, or the previous owner died of some dreaded disease. In short, the property comes with a handicap because many people would feel uncomfortable spending any time in the house. The problem here is that there is no way to "fix" the problem. Only time will obliterate the stigma. Unless you plan to demolish the structure or change the use considerably, such properties should not be considered. Of course, if you plan to live there a long time and don't mind being the neighborhood "weirdo," then you probably will get a good deal.

32

THE INSPECTION

It is common practice to do a walk-through inspection and hire a professional inspector prior to buying a home. Such due diligence is even more compelling when buying a property that is offered for sale at a below-market price. By its nature, such a home has some drawback that reduces its market appeal. It is the investor's task to find out what that is and assess the remedy.

Much can be accomplished with a cursory examination of the property, even if you are not highly knowledgeable about construction techniques and quality. You probably will not want to have every property under consideration professionally inspected. Instead, you will need some type of winnowing process to eliminate the ones that do not fit your strategy. Let the pros look at the ones that appear acceptable to the untrained eye.

How you evaluate a property depends on, first, whether you will live in the home or use it for income production, and second, how much you can afford to invest in turning the property around. If you are looking for a personal residence, you will look at the property primarily from the standpoint of your personal preferences and needs. If the home has some unique quality that you value, you may go to greater lengths to correct the things you do not like. On the other hand, if the property will be rented out or sold back into the market, your objective is to make it safe (compliant with local codes) and attractive to the typical end-user. Likewise, if the property is selling for a large discount compared to similar homes in market-ready condition, you can afford to do more drastic rehabilitation.

At the first examination of the property, try to detect

the existence of flaws that are basically *incurable*. These are things that cannot be changed in any practical sense, yet have a detrimental effect on the property's value. If the property has any of these problems, it should be rejected unless the price is extremely low:

- Noisy, crime-ridden, and disruptive neighborhood (unless there is an active and substantial renovation movement ongoing and you think it will turn the area around).
- A neighborhood that is in transition away from residential (unless you are buying the property for the land and plan to change the use).
- Area where surrounding homes are not maintained.
- An awkward floor plan. Think about the routine functions around the home and how they would be accomplished with this layout.
- Structural type. A large home with several stories will not be as popular as a one-story house of the same size. However, in some locations, a two-story house that provides a small garden or yard may be preferable to one that consumes the whole site.
- Lack of site size or awkward orientation on the site. Unless you can buy surrounding land parcels, you cannot change this situation.

Next, look for things that can be changed or corrected, but require substantial expense to do so. These flaws are not necessarily fatal, but might eliminate any property except the deepest discounted homes. One problem with taking on these types of properties is the difficulty of fully assessing the cost of repairs. Indeed, many of these problems can be much worse than they first appear. In general, problems in the following areas should eliminate all but the lowest priced properties:

- Drainage (may require extensive landscaping and underground channeling; may be hard to find a spot where excess water can drain to; may have already caused extensive structural damage).

- Water leaks (can be hard to stop; may indicate drainage or guttering problems; may indicate more serious structural damage).
- Inadequate electrical service (may require extensive rewiring; may coincide with inadequate outlets and lighting for modern usage).
- Foundation damage (hard to tell how extensive without tearing into house; need to fix cause as well as damage).
- Ventilation (may be caused with orientation of house relative to prevailing winds; may require new windows; places undue burden on heating and air conditioning equipment).
- Hazards such as lead paint, asbestos ceilings and insulation, and radon (detection may require special tests; may not be too much of a problem but could complicate resale if not eliminated; elimination often costly).
- Lack of trees (it takes a long time to cultivate trees from saplings and mature trees are expensive and do not transplant easily).

Finally, there may be items that need attention, and will not cost a significant sum, yet fall within the category of things that normally must be replaced at some point in most homes. Therefore, the existence of these problems should be noted and used in negotiating a price, but should not eliminate the house from consideration:

- Worn roof covering (if not leaking; a leaky roof requires closer examination of roof and attic structure).
- Outdated or faulty bath and kitchen fixtures and equipment (minor remodeling of these rooms is one of the most cost-efficient upgrades available).
- Unattractive or worn-out paint and floor coverings (relatively minor investment here can make big difference in appeal).

- Broken windows and doors.
- Outmoded or cheap hardware (installing better doorknobs and light fixtures can improve market appeal).
- Old, undersized, or inefficient heating and air conditioning equipment (expensive but can improve comfort while lowering operating expenses).
- Dead lawn and lack of landscaping.

Price out solutions to any of these problems that are apparent and factor that estimate into your offer. The seller may not agree that these are problems. That is the signal to find another property.

33

CONTRACT OR SWEAT EQUITY?

One way to buy a house at an attractive price is to take on the responsibility of a property that needs repair or remodeling, or both. Unfortunately, paying someone to fix up the property may negate any reduction in price you were able to negotiate. Traditionally, people with more time than money have been attracted to the "handyman's special" because they could invest "sweat equity" (time and the willingness to spend it making improvements and repairs) to bringing the property up to some acceptable standard of quality and condition. However, there is a limit to what the layman should undertake. Some repairs require specialized equipment and knowledge and, if not done properly, can render the property even less appealing and may even be dangerous.

Knowing what you can accomplish using your own efforts is important to two decisions. First, whether you do the work yourself or contract it out may affect how much you offer for the property. If the work requires professional attention, you may need a larger discount to make the deal work. Second, if you decide to buy the home, knowing how much work will need to be done professionally will help you put together a rehab plan.

Here are the major factors that should impact the evaluation:

Time. Do you plan to do the work in the spare time leftover from a job and other life responsibilities? Do you plan to live on the property while completing the work? If free time is limited or there are things that must be completed quickly to make the property habitable, you may need to use some hired help. Unless you are experienced in the building trades, many of these tasks will take longer than anticipated. And there is always the possibility of finding bigger problems in the course of making a repair.

Knowledge and skill. If you must learn how to do each task, the work will take more time and the results may not be totally satisfactory. For some people, this is fine. They use the first house they tackle as a learning experience and are content to live with, or take the time to fix, their mistakes. If you are more critical, you may want to avoid doing anything that shows. In general, if the property will be used by tenants, your first concern should be durability. If it is for personal use, your first concern may be appearance and convenience. If you have time, but knowledge is limited, you may be able to work out an arrangement with a professional contractor under which you do much of the preparation work, tearing out the old material and cleaning up the site, for example, prior to the professionals coming in and completing the job. That could save quite a bit of costs and still result in a high-quality rehab. Be aware than many remodeling and rehabilitation jobs require building code permits and inspections. In many cases, the regulations require licensed tradesman to do the work.

Temperament. Some people do not mind plodding along on a long-term project, content with the gradual progress being made. Others like to get in the heat of the battle and complete a job while the juices are flowing. Many of the things required to rehab a property are of the long-term type, especially when you are doing them yourself. Of course, bringing in teams of professionals will speed up the work. The slow approach gives you time to evaluate the effect of the change and to decide on how you want it done. The quick approach requires you to decide much of this beforehand and any changes in midstream must be decided without much deliberation.

Financing. Obviously, how you finance the work is

critical as well. The term "sweat equity" implies very little in the way of cash expense, but that is misleading. Even for do-it-yourselfers, there will be considerable costs for materials, tools, and, possibly, government permits. If you have the luxury of time, these costs may be met through periodic use of available cash, a tax refund, or a bonus here and there. If the job must be done on schedule, there probably will be a need for some financing to make sure materials are available when needed. Financing imposes a cost of its own and affects scheduling, because the costs increase as the project is drawn out.

There are a number of ways to finance rehab. Self-financing can be done in conjunction with the gradual improvement approach. Unsecured loans, even credit card debt, can be used for small to moderate expenses. A home improvement loan, in the form of a second mortgage, could be used. These types of loans tend to be expensive, so that there is a strong incentive to repay them as soon as possible. It could be possible to refinance the house after rehab at a higher loan amount to retire both the original purchase mortgage and the improvement loan. Hopefully, your efforts at rehab will raise the market value of the home enough to support the larger loan. A home equity loan might be used, but this option probably will not be available unless you have significant equity in the property. In other words, if you purchased with a low-down-payment loan, you will not have sufficient equity to get much of a home equity loan. However, if it is feasible, such loans carry interest rates not much higher than first mortgages. There probably would be no need to refinance. For certain borrowers, there are loans that can be used for both purchase and rehab. If you are eligible, this may be your best choice. More detail is provided in the next Key.

34

FINANCING PURCHASE AND REHABILITATION

Buying a house that needs substantial work can provide a bargain, but financing the venture may be tricky. A conventional lender will base the loan on the current value of the property. To finance the rehab work, you will need to get a home improvement loan or a nonmortgage loan (if you do the work yourself, you may be able to buy materials with a credit card), then refinance the first mortgage when the work is completed. Hopefully, the house will appraise high enough so that the new loan will cover the rehab expenses.

If you don't mind doing some paperwork, there may be a better way. The Federal Housing Administration (FHA), a part of the Department of Housing and Urban Development, has a program that makes available special loans that combine purchase and rehab. With one of these loans, you can buy a home with a mortgage based on the house's value *after* rehab is complete. You do have to comply with a set of requirements and submit cost estimates and plans to the FHA, but the result can save the expense of getting high-cost home improvement financing and of refinancing the first mortgage later.

The FHA doesn't make loans, but insures private lenders who make the loans. If the borrower defaults, the FHA will step in to reimburse the lender's costs of foreclosing the loan. The most popular insurance program is the 203(b) program, which insures low-down-payment loans on modestly priced homes. The rehab program, 203(k), works the same way, except the loan includes rehab and remodeling expenses. The loans are made by private lenders, approved by the FHA to do this kind of business. (For information about the program and a list of approved lenders, go to the HUD Web site, *http://www.hud.gov/fha/sfh/sfhrehab.html*).

The 203(k) program is intended for single-family homes. However, the FHA includes homes with one to four units in that category. In fact, the agency is somewhat broad in what qualifies, including:

- Up to four dwelling units, as long as they are attached. No separate apartment in the backyard.
- A demolished building, as long as some of the foundation is used in reconstruction.
- Conversion of one big house into up to four units or conversion of a multi-unit building into a single-family structure.
- Purchase of a house and separate land and moving the house to the land.
- A residential property with a limited amount of nonresidential space. However, the loan will pay only for work on the residential parts of the property.
- Up to four condominium units, as long as they are in one structure. Townhouses also qualify if they are separated by effective firewalls. Special requirements apply to condominium properties. In addition, the borrower must occupy one of the units.

Using the loan to buy and rehab a property is only one way it can be used. You can use it to buy a property and a house on another site and to pay for moving the house and setting it on a foundation on the purchased property. Further, you can use the loan to refinance an existing mortgage on a home you own that needs rehabilitation.

Here's what the FHA requires:

- The home is a one- to four-unit structure.
- The home is at least one year old.
- The property must conform to local zoning ordinances.
- Rehab work must cost at least $5,000.
- Eligible rehab work includes repair of existing

structures, additions to the structure such as added rooms or a garage, updating of obsolete space and equipment, and remodeling. The agency is especially receptive to improvements that eliminate health and safety hazards.

- Cosmetic and minor repairs may be covered but only if they are in excess of the minimum $5,000 amount allocated to major rehab work.
- All new and remodeled spaces must conform to stated energy conservation standards. For example, adequate weatherproofing must be part of the work. Also, any replacement equipment must be energy-efficient.

Here is how the program works. When a contract to purchase (in the case of purchase and rehab) has been signed, you find an approved FHA 203(k) lender and make an application. In addition to the usual loan application, the lender will require documents describing the work that will done and how much it will cost. As part of loan processing, the lender may commission an "as is" appraisal to estimate what the property is worth before rehab. A value-after-rehabilitation appraisal will be made as well. The loan amount is based on the lesser of the "as is" value plus costs of rehab and 110 percent of the value after rehabilitation estimate. When the loan is approved, a special escrow account is established containing the proceeds of the loan earmarked for rehab. This account can be drawn upon as the work progresses. The FHA requires inspections along the way before these draws can be made. Also, 10 percent of each draw is held back to make sure no workmen's liens are placed on the property.

All this oversight and deliberation may not seem appealing. And for some, it may prove too cumbersome and limited to work. However, the program is intended to result in a quality addition to the housing stock and to help energetic people get into a home of their own. If you feel that working with such a program will not jeopardize your plans, the FHA 203(k) program may be just the ticket.

35

LOCAL GOVERNMENT RESTRICTIONS

If you plan to physically change the property that you acquire, you will undoubtedly confront several local government laws that affect how you proceed. Although in some locations, such laws are not in effect or are not diligently enforced, many localities take these matters very seriously and failure to comply can lead to additional expense, delay, and even criminal penalties. In fact, it is best to become familiar with local requirements prior to committing to a particular property.

Local governments do not pass such laws merely to harass citizens who want to improve their property. The laws serve the purpose of trying to assure that structures do not pose threats to public health and safety and that land uses that might interfere with one another are not in close proximity. Blanket restrictions, as well as private covenants placed in property deeds, help to make an area more compatible to residential use. And whereas everyone may have a different concept of a pleasant residential setting, the law must establish one standard for all. That is why the standards exist as minimum requirements. Anything over the minimum is left to individual taste or private covenant.

For renovation work, two types of local restrictions are most important: zoning and building codes. Zoning affects how a property is used. It is intended to keep incompatible uses separated. It comes into play if you want to change the use of the property, such as convert a single-family home into a duplex. It may also be relevant if you want to enlarge a structure or build additional structures on the lot. Building codes are used to prevent substandard construction. You may need to comply with building codes if you construct something new, rebuild, enlarge, or remodel an existing structure.

Zoning. The zoning ordinance affects how properties are used. In many cases, this not only refers to the type of activities (residential, commercial, industrial) but also to the intensity of use. In other words, homes on quarter-acre lots may have a different zone than those on two-acre lots and a different zone for apartment buildings. Consequently, you may need to apply for rezoning if you:

- Enlarge a house by adding rooms or increasing its height. Most zoning ordinances have set back, side yard, and height restrictions.
- Convert a single-family to a multi-family home. Possibly, you may need authorization to go the opposite way; converting a multi-family structure to a single-family home.
- Use a single-family home for group housing or as a day-care center.
- Convert a house to commercial uses, such as a hair salon shop or a tax preparation service.

It is also a good idea to check the zoning map to determine if the current use is in conformance. When a zoning ordinance is passed or revised, some existing uses may not conform to the law. These property owners are given time to remove the "nonconforming" uses. In most cases, these uses can remain but cannot be substantially rehabilitated or reconstructed. If you buy a nonconforming use, you may have a surprise when it comes time to apply for a permit.

Zoning is exercised by municipal governments but may also apply to areas within a mile or so of the city limits. In some states, cities have "extra-jurisdictional territory" authority that extends beyond the city boundaries. All the area under the city's control is classified by a particular "zone" that lists the types of uses and densities allowed in that zone. The city planning office maintains a map showing the location of these zones. The zoning ordinance defines permitted uses in each zone.

If what you want to do with the property does not comply with the current classification, you can appeal to the city to change the classification. This is called a "rezoning request" and you apply for it at the city clerk's office. These applications are reviewed by the planning department and the planning and zoning commission. The commission and the city counsel will hold public hearings to allow citizens to object or support your proposal. The city counsel then approves or rejects your request. If you cannot get rezoning, you may be able to get a variance or a special use permit. You have to show that the current restriction makes it impossible or impractical to use your property.

Some zoning ordinances establish a hierarchy of land uses, with the least intensive at the top and the most intensive at the bottom. For each zone, a use that is higher in the hierarchy than the use allowed is also allowed. So, for example, you would not need a rezoning to convert a duplex into a single-family home, as long as the duplex is a conforming use. The ordinances are called "cumulative" and are in contrast to "exclusive" zoning, which only allows the uses proscribed in the ordinance for each zone.

Building permits. Any type of construction or significant remodeling will require a building permit. Like zoning, these permits are primarily a function of municipalities, but in some states, counties may be authorized as well. Contact the building inspector's office in the city where the property is located to get information on requirements and application procedures.

In general, here is how building permits work. Prior to construction or remodeling, you would take a plan showing all the work that will be done and file an application at the building inspection office. There will be a nominal fee depending on how much work will be done.

The office will check to see if the proposed structure is in compliance with the zoning ordinance and other laws. The city will have a set of construction standards to which the work must conform. For example, the building code may require wall studs at 18-inch intervals or so many electrical outlets per room or the installation of drain cleanouts in the plumbing system.

There will be a series of inspections that apply to new construction. For remodeling, only the systems being worked on need be inspected. Any failure to pass an inspection requires the owner to bring the work into compliance. When all inspections have been successfully completed, the owner can apply for a "certificate of occupancy" that states that the structure may be safely occupied.

Other permits. There may be other permits that affect your plans for reconstruction or rehabilitation:

- Demolition permit. Cities often require a permit to take down a structure. Basically, this is required to assure that utilities have been shut off prior to demolition.
- Driveway permits. Some cities require a permit to build or rebuild a driveway or walkway abutting the street. The usual safety concerns apply.
- Moving permit. A permit may be required for moving a structure on the public roads. Along with the permit comes assistance in selecting the best route.

If you anticipate that a property will require more than cosmetic remodeling, you should find out as much as possible about how local laws will affect your plans. Many cities have prepared convenient brochures and booklets explaining local development laws and who to contact. You may also have luck finding information on the Internet by accessing the city government Web page.

36

SPECIAL PROGRAMS FOR QUALIFIED HOME BUYERS

Local, state, and federal governments have expressed concern over two related problems: the decline of inner-city neighborhoods and the lack of affordable housing. Often the two concerns coincide in special programs aimed at helping people buy homes or improve the homes they own in depressed areas of the city. If you qualify for one of these programs or if you are willing to live in an area pinpointed by the city, you may be able to acquire a good home for low cost.

These programs have a variety of things to offer. Some actually provide houses at low prices. Others provide special financing with below-market interest rates and favorable terms. A few promise to lower other homeownership costs, such as property taxes. All of these programs are focused and administered largely at the local level. Therefore, they may not be available in your area and, when available, may have features quite different from those in other areas. Here we provide a general overview of the types of programs you may encounter and show how to find out more.

Urban homesteading. Do you recall reading about the homesteading programs that settled the American West? Anyone willing to carve out and work a farm in the new territory could claim the land for free or a nominal amount. Some cities have similar programs for anyone willing to live in specific parts of the city. The city deeds over the home for a nominal amount to an individual for use as his/her home. The homes usually have been acquired by the city for back taxes and may require repair and rehabilitation. There may be, as well, restrictions on who can acquire the homes. The "buyer" may be required to bring the home up to code standards and live in the home for a specified period. Additionally, there may be some restrictions on resale. If interested, check with the mayor's or city manager's office in the locality for program availability.

Mortgage revenue bond programs. More ubiquitous than homesteading is the mortgage revenue bond program that provides special financing for first-time home buyers. Bargain financing is the next best thing to a bargain price on the house. And you may be able to get both, if the home is in an area targeted for renewal by the city. The mortgage bond program provides special mortgage loans at interest rates significantly below the going rate in the market. The loans are offered by local lending institutions (banks, savings and loans, mortgage bankers) who sell the loans to a local or state housing finance agency. The agency raises funds by issuing municipal bonds. Because these bonds are exempt from federal income taxation, the agencies can borrow at rates lower than those available to private mortgage lenders. The low rate is passed on to the borrower.

The catch is that the borrower must fit certain characteristics, including not having owned a home for the past three years. There may be income and house price limits that vary by locality. If you fit this description, you can buy a home anywhere in the jurisdiction. If not, you still may be able to get a loan if willing to buy a home in areas targeted by the city, usually in inner-city neighborhoods. In some cases, investors are allowed to participate when buying homes in the target areas.

Some areas have programs that provide assistance for down payments and closing costs that work in conjunction with the mortgage bond program. Usually, these are restricted to the lowest income categories eligible for assistance. To find out more about program availability, contact the housing finance agency for the locality or, as often is the case outside the largest cities, the state housing finance agency. Information on loan availability may be had, as well, from local lenders participating in the program.

Mortgage credit certificates. This program is an alternative to the mortgage revenue bond program and operates with the same qualifications and requirements. The difference is in the form of assistance provided. Instead of a below-market interest rate, the home buyer receives a certificate that allows the buyer to claim a credit on federal income taxes each year. The credit is equal to 35 percent of interest paid on the loan, up to a maximum of the total taxes due or $2,000, whichever is lower. A tax credit reduces the **tax bill** dollar for dollar, so the certificate could mean up to $2,000 in cash assistance each year for the home buyer.

Affordable housing programs. During the 1990s, the federal government and a number of local governments created programs to improve access to housing for those with below median incomes. The ingredients in these programs vary greatly: production of low-cost housing, rent subsidies, special financing, cash assistance to buyers, and technical assistance for those who need to repair their homes. Often, the programs are coordinated through a local office of affordable housing or some similar title. Check locally to find out availability and requirements.

There are a number of efforts conducted by nongovernmental groups; generally nonprofit altruistic or religious organizations devoted to affordable housing or inner-city renewal. Of note is the program run by Habitat for Humanity. The organization builds new homes with volunteer labor and donated materials for those that qualify. Beneficiaries are required to contribute to the construction effort. There often is special financing to make the home even more affordable.

Enterprise zones. Another effort to stimulate economic activity in depressed areas is a program that applies special rules to those areas. For the type of activities desired, the city may relax regulatory requirements, waive normally required fees, and provide property tax breaks. The activities usually are oriented toward employers and businesses, but home buyers may come in for special treatment under some programs. Check with the city administration.

37

SHOULD YOU PARTICIPATE IN AUCTIONS?

When markets are slow and foreclosures abound, inevitably there will be a number of large real estate auctions. Holders of REO periodically turn to auctions to help clear their inventories. The auction process is a good way to attract a number of willing buyers and to assure sales of properties.

Should you, as an individual investor or home buyer, participate in this process? You may think that bidding at an auction is for professionals who are savvy to the ways of auctioneers and that a novice may get lost in the flurry of activity at a typical bidding session. To some extent this is true. You do need to know something about the way auctions are conducted. However, it is even more important to know the property that you are bidding on and what its maximum value is to you. It is also important to exercise some self control so that you do not get carried away in the pursuit of a popular parcel.

But that doesn't mean you should avoid auctions. Indeed, some of the best bargains have been obtained at auctions, and by people with very little experience in buying real estate.

Auctions have long carried the stigma of property dumping. The general feeling is that if you can't sell a property through normal channels, you put it up for auction. Maybe this is a carryover from the special auction used at foreclosure sales. However, public auctions are different. The method is commonly used for such commodities as art works and agricultural products, and these sales techniques often produce spectacular sale prices.

Generally, holders of real property resort to auctions because they think that the property will not increase in value over time and that waiting for a normal sale is not worth the carrying costs. To that extent, the properties offered may be had for bargain prices. However, knowledgeable sellers know that an auction may produce the highest price possible for a property. They are hoping that there will be enough bidding activity from motivated buyers to result in a sale at maximum value.

In reality, when a large number of properties are sold at auction, many do go for prices above their market value. At the same time, several sell for truly bargain prices. It depends on how much competition there is for each property.

For many properties, there is no way to tell how much they are worth. Their original sales price, in the case of previously owned properties, is no guide in a depressed market. You can make a determination, but it requires doing some homework: inspecting the property and checking with current sales of comparable properties. If you are willing to do this background checking, you will be prepared to bid intelligently for the properties you want.

Other Keys in this section will help you prepare. You will find information on how to find auction opportunities, how auctions work, how to prepare, and what you may end up with if you bid.

38

FINDING AUCTION OPPORTUNITIES

From a real estate marketing standpoint, auctions are major events. Unless foreclosures are especially heavy, auctions are not conducted frequently. Therefore, you will need to keep apprised of upcoming auctions and be prepared to act when they take place.

Auction companies know that attracting a sizable crowd is the key to generating high sales prices. Consequently, a lot of effort goes into promoting the event. Look for ads in the real estate section of the local newspaper. Call auction companies or institutions that hold REO (often the auctioneers are not local, especially if the area is not a large city). If an auction is planned, they should be able to provide you with a brochure or list of properties. These properties should be open for inspection prior to the sale.

In areas where a lot of inventory is sold by auction, special publications have developed to inform buyers of opportunities. These publications list properties that are for sale by owners who have acquired the property through foreclosure. You can subscribe to these services or purchase individual copies of the publications.

You may prefer to operate through a real estate broker. Often, brokers can earn commissions if someone they register at an auction buys a property. Advise your broker of your interest in property auctions and let him or her keep you informed of upcoming opportunities. The broker will probably make it easier to inspect properties before the sale.

A growing avenue for publicizing events is the Internet. A key word search will reveal a host of auction companies operating throughout the country.

39

HOW AN AUCTION WORKS

Once you decide to participate in an auction, you should understand how auctions are conducted. There are different types of auctions. They vary in the way bids are placed, in the way a winning bid is awarded, and in the scope of what is offered at auction. Almost all real estate auctions begin with a minimum bid suggested by the auctioneer. Bids from the audience are taken until no one is willing to outbid the last, highest bid. After a brief period, the property is awarded to the highest bidder. If no one is willing to bid the minimum price, the property may be re-entered at a lower starting point or may go unsold. When a large number of properties are offered at auction, the entire bidding process for each property may last only a few minutes.

An important consideration is whether any reservations are placed on the bidding process. An absolute auction awards the property to the highest bidder no matter what the winning bid is. In this way, the seller is assured the property will be sold (unless there are no bids at all), and the bidders are assured of getting the property at the winning bid price.

Some sellers are uncomfortable with the idea of selling at any price and may insist on a minimum bid. In this case, if no one places a bid at least as high as the minimum, the property will not be sold. This may happen when a seller is unsure of the market and is willing to hold the property if it does not bring a specified price. It may also be evidence that the seller does not completely trust the auction process, particularly when the turnout is lower than expected. (Sometimes a minimum is enforced by the courts in foreclosure sales to protect the defaulting borrower from abuse by the lender.)

The most restricted auctions are those with unstated reservation prices (Dutch or one-sided auctions). The seller can decide after the bidding whether or not to accept the highest bid. There is some question, when this tactic is used, as to whether the seller really wanted to sell or merely get a feel for the market value of the property. You may not want to participate in auctions where the highest bid can be turned down.

It is also instructive to know the scope of the auction. A stand-alone auction typically deals with only one property. This is rare, except in the case of foreclosure sales. Single-owner auctions are very common. Holders of REO or developers may conduct an auction covering all or a portion of their inventory. In general, these auctions do not employ reservations or minimum bids and the policies for bidding on each property are uniform. A multiple-owner auction may be used when several owners join together because their holdings are not large enough to justify individual auctions. In such auctions, there is a greater possibility that reservations will be placed on some properties.

In the end, your decision to participate in an auction will hinge on the quality of the properties included and any additional considerations included. For example, the seller may have arranged for financing to be offered on properties sold.

40

TIPS FOR BIDDING AT AN AUCTION

The key to getting an auction bargain is knowing the properties you are bidding on, having a reservation price for each property, and avoiding getting caught up in the bidding frenzy. These principles should prevent you from paying too high a price for a property you expected to be a bargain (the point of going to the auction in the first place).

Knowing the properties means actually investigating each property you are interested in. Prior to the sale, you can obtain a list of properties that will be sold. You should have an opportunity to visit the properties. You should spend the same effort you would if you were making an offer on the property through a negotiated sales contract. If the location and other features are desirable, you may even employ a professional inspector to check over the property. If the property is a condominium, you may want to look at the legal papers that affect what you can do within the unit and the common property. (Some condos may preclude leasing out units.)

Armed with the information you find in your investigations, you can form an opinion of the property's value. This will be the basis for your reservation price, the highest price you will bid at the auction. The opening bid, the original price, and any other value information obtained at the auction are not adequate guides to how much you should pay for the property. You must form your own idea of its value.

When the actual bidding opens, the auctioneer will usually set a starting bid. This bid is set at least 30–40 percent below the expected price for the property (or market value). The auctioneer will try to generate bidding enthusiasm by encouraging higher bids. There may be required increments by which the current bid must be raised. In some cases, it is possible to enter written bids before the auction starts. In this way, you can bid on property without having to be present at the auction. These bids are entered by the auctioneer and are valid until someone out-bids the entry. If no bids exceed the written bid, the submitter wins the property at a price one increment above the next highest bid.

When bidding is active, there is a tendency for the price to rise quickly. Unless you absolutely must have the property, you should stick to your reservation price even if it means losing out. Remember that your purpose is to get a bargain. The effect of active bidding in a good auction is what causes bid prices to be at or even higher than market value appraisals for many properties.

It is always possible that bidding will be tepid enough on some properties so that an uninformed bidder can end up with a good deal. However, when bidding is active, there is no substitute for adequate preparation. There are no good guidelines in the bidding process to tell you how much you should bid. You must know how much the property is worth to you. It is no disgrace (nor a waste of time) to go home empty-handed.

41

PAYING FOR YOUR AUCTION BUY

Being the winning bidder for the property you want is great, but you still have to finance the purchase. At the bottom of a market cycle, some buyers are able to buy so cheaply that they can pay cash or put the purchase on their credit cards. You are not likely to find such conditions very often. When you do, it may be because the property will require a lot of additional costs or will not produce income for some time.

Financing an auction purchase may be a bit more tricky than other purchases. You may need to pre-arrange credit before the auction. Most auctions allow a certain amount of time for buyers to line up their financing, recognizing that lenders require a specific piece of property to be identified before approving a loan. However, if your application is turned down, you will probably forfeit your deposit.

You should familiarize yourself with all regulations of the auction beforehand. Many require bidders to have a cashier's check or certified check for at least $500 before allowing them to enter the bidding area. Winning bidders may need to come up with some percentage of the price shortly after the auction. Find out what is required for you to bid and how much time, if any, is provided for loan approval.

Some auction sellers offer financing as a way to attract more bidders. The loans are usually provided at favorable terms compared to the market, often with a low down payment or no credit check. This is especially the case when the properties being offered are modestly priced homes. The sellers are hoping to attract home buyers. Seller financing makes the financing problem much less troublesome. Find out what is offered before attending. Factor any financing terms into your reservation price. You can afford to pay a higher price if financing is included at below-market rates.

42

SHOULD YOU WORK WITH AN AGENT?

Real estate markets are often hard to get a handle on. Most properties are unique in some important ways that are not immediately apparent. The attractiveness, and thus value, of specific locations may vary over time. If you are not involved in the market frequently, you cannot gather and maintain the information necessary to help you reach an informed decision.

Real estate brokers and salespeople are involved in the market frequently and can be an excellent source of information. It makes sense to use their services when they can help you find the best deal. This is especially true when the service comes at no direct cost to you. (Some may argue that you are paying for this service whether you use it or not.)

Brokers and salespeople can be very useful in finding properties. Many foreclosed or bargain homes are sold like any other home, through exclusive listing contracts and the Multiple Listing Service (see Key 43). The broker can provide access to this inventory. If the property is being sold by a government agency, a broker or a salesperson may assist you in making a bid, using the proper procedure and form. A broker may even represent you or accompany you to an auction.

For most people wanting to buy real estate, especially those with a day job, the question is not whether to use a broker or a salesperson but how many to use. Brokers and salespeople are in the business on a daily basis. They talk with buyers and sellers regularly and with other brokers and salespeople in their own firm and others that they deal with. By working with brokers or salespeople, you can tap into their network of contacts and knowledge of markets and properties. In fact, if you intend to be an active trader of properties, you may want to develop a rapport with an agent knowledgeable about the part of town or properties that interest you.

When you have more than one broker or salesperson helping you look, the first agent who shows you the property that you end up buying will earn a commission (some states use a procuring clause: the agent that writes the offer earns the commission). Some agents will want a buyer to work with them exclusively and will explain that they won't expend a great deal of effort if the buyer is also working with another agent. However, if the buyer is interested in more than one property and/or feels that the broker isn't providing enough service to deserve an exclusive, the buyer should feel free to go elsewhere.

Since the early 1990s, there has been a growing movement to provide to buyers and sellers a statement disclosing just whom the broker represents. This "agency disclosure" has spawned a trend whereby brokers (or salespeople) represent buyers, trying to get a buyer the very best possible deal. This includes not only the price but also the terms of the sale, including closing date, repairs, personal property included in the sale, and so on. Most often, the broker, even a "buyer's broker," is paid by the seller. If a fee is taken from both parties, it must be disclosed. If you prefer to work with an agent professing to represent you, the buyer, go ahead. Recognize, however, that most agents will provide you with the same information on properties on the market and help you work up an offer, regardless of whom they legally represent.

43

BROKERS, SALESPEOPLE, REALTORS®, MULTIPLE LISTINGS

Most laymen are not familiar with the precise terminology of the real estate brokerage business. All 50 states in the United States have licensing requirements for the real estate industry. They license brokers, salespeople, and appraisers.

In most states, the entry level is a "salesperson" or "salesman." To become one, a candidate must meet the state's requirements, which vary from state to state. Requirements generally include education in real estate (generally at least a 30-hour course) and passing a 2- to 3-hour, 80- to 100-question multiple-choice examination. A salesperson must also be sponsored by a licensed broker.

Although broker licensing requirements vary greatly from state to state, a broker candidate generally must have had experience (usually two to three years) as an active salesperson, must take further course work, and must pass a more rigorous examination. Brokers are responsible for the actions of salespeople they sponsor. Brokers can do certain things that salespeople cannot. In most states, a broker's license is required for someone who helps another buy, sell, list, or lease real estate. The salesperson works as an agent for the broker; the broker is an agent of the buyer or seller.

In many situations, a broker will sponsor several salespeople. The broker may provide office space, telephone facilities, training sessions, and so on, for the sponsored salespeople. Commission splits between the broker and salesperson often depend on the volume of business generated by the salesperson and the level of service provided by the broker.

Approximately one of three real estate brokers and salespeople are members of the National Association of Realtors® (NAR). These people pay dues to NAR and also to the state and local associations of Realtors®. A licensed broker or salesperson who is also a member of NAR may prefer to be called a Realtor®, which is a registered trademark of NAR. A real estate broker or salesperson who is not a member of NAR may not be called a Realtor®.

Important to buyers and sellers in many cities is the presence of a multiple listing service (MLS). Often these are organized and run by the local board of Realtors®. Members of the MLS are required to enter all their listings into the MLS system within a short period of time—typically 48 to 72 hours. For a buyer or seller, the MLS instantly exposes the property to most of the active participants in the market. With the aid of an MLS member, a potential buyer or seller is exposed to this great information and data network.

44

SALES CONTRACTS

In most Northeastern states a *binder* is used to make an initial offer. When accepted, the owner agrees to take the property off the market and have an attorney prepare, in the next few days, a contract for the sale of the property.

In other parts of the country, a *sales contract* formalizes the negotiation process between you and the seller. This form is called a *contract of sale, agreement of sale,* or *earnest money* contract in different parts of the United States.

To make a binding offer, you must use a written contract. Contracts for the sale of real estate must be in writing to be enforceable. Besides, the seller can't respond in any meaningful way to a verbal offer because there are so many details to be arranged. If you are working through a broker or agent, he or she will have pre-printed standard contract forms. In some states the exact wording of the form is determined by the state agency that regulates professional real estate licenses, called the real estate commission. As an alternative, you could have an attorney draft a contract for you. However, the standard forms cover the most common items needed for the sale of a house.

You should realize that once you submit an offer in the form of a sales contract, the seller may accept your offer by signing the contract. The contract then becomes binding on both you and the seller. If the seller counter-offers, it will most likely be in the form of modifications to the contract you submitted. A counter-offer is legally a rejection of the offer and a substitution of a new offer. The counter-offer becomes binding when you initial all changes made. Negotiations become more difficult if you begin to add new requirements to the contract. Therefore, when you make your first offer, you should be careful to include all items you want in the contract.

If you have never seen a sales contract, this discussion may be a little confusing. The contract states the price you are willing to pay for the home, but it also covers all conditions attached to the sale. Remember that the price is only one point in the negotiation of a sale. Agreement must be reached on how the price is met, timing of the sale, what is included in the sale, who pays selling and financing costs, the move-in dates, and under what conditions either party can back out of the sale.

All contracts identify the seller and buyer, the property involved, and the offered price. References to the property should include a legal description and identify what is to be included (any furnishings? mineral rights?). Price should be elaborated by stating the amount of cash down payment, money to be provided through a mortgage loan, and any money paid immediately as a deposit (earnest money).

The reason financing provisions are important is that most contracts include a contingency provision in case you are turned down for the loan. If you can't get the loan, this clause allows you to recover your earnest money. At the same time, it frees the seller to offer the home to another buyer. Generally, there are separate forms for conventional, FHA, and VA financing. The seller needs to know the type of financing, since some loans require the seller to pay discount points. The type of financing used may affect the price and other points of negotiation.

Other contingencies may be placed in the contract for the protection of the buyer. You probably want to condition the sale on the property successfully passing inspections for physical condition and absence of wood destroying insects, especially termites. These provisions give you the right to have the property inspected (at your expense). If anything is found wrong, the seller has the option of repairing the problem or, if too costly, releasing you from the contract. You may also require the right to void the sale if the property is found to be in a flood prone (hazard) area. If you own a home currently, you may make the sale contingent on selling your home. The seller may have the right to accept back-up contracts from other potential buyers. If the seller finds another buyer while the property is under contract to you subject to a contingency, you may be allowed 48 hours to delete the contingency and agree to close in coming days, or the seller will have the right to sell to the other party.

The contract sets a date for the closing and identifies who is responsible for the various expenses of sale. The latter provision is important if these expenses are not handled in the customary way. For example, if you want the seller to pay for discount points or if you are offering to pay the broker's commission, it should be stated in the contract. What is written in a contract is what matters. Verbal promises vanish into thin air. If you do not understand a provision in the contract at any point in the negotiation, ask your broker or attorney to explain it. Make sure the explanation fits. Many brokers will not admit that they do not understand a provision in a preprinted contract. Once signed, the contract will dictate how the sale is conducted and determine how much you pay and what you will get. No changes are allowed in the contract unless the other party agrees to them.

45

NEGOTIATION

One of the keys to buying real estate is good negotiation. In the United States most prices are set by the seller, but this is not the case for real estate. Consequently, participants in a real estate transaction are often unfamiliar and uncomfortable with the bargaining process. Of course, you could accept the other party's offer and complete the transaction quickly, but that would be to your financial detriment and regret.

When negotiation a price, both seller and buyer should have an idea of their *reservation prices*. This is the minimum price the seller will accept or the maximum price the buyer can pay. If you are the seller, your reservation price may be *market value*. You figure you can get this price on the market if the deal falls through. If you are the buyer, your reservation price will be *investment value*. This is how much the property is worth to you, considering your personal situation.

The seller will add a margin to his or her reservation price, while the buyer will subtract a margin to start the bargaining. This gives each party some bargaining room. Each hopes to get a better deal than the reservation price, if possible. Whether the seller or buyer has to come close to the reservation price depends on competition in the market. If there are lots of properties on the market, the buyer is in a good position and may extract concessions from the seller. If there are lots of buyers and few good properties, the seller can insist on the reservation price. You should be aware of the competitive condition of the market when negotiating.

Bargaining starts when the buyer makes an offer for the property. The seller may accept or reject this offer, but usually comes back with a counter offer at a higher price. The buyer then responds with another offer. The process continues until either both parties agree to terms or negotiations stop because of an impasse. Often in this process of offer and counter-offer, terms of sale other than price come into play. Either party may give in on price in return for concessions on other terms. In the process, you should keep in mind your reservation price (in terms of total costs) and try to move the negotiations toward the form of deal that best fits your situation.

Virtually everything in a property transaction is negotiable. This means not only the price but other terms such as:

- The form of payment (all cash at closing, deferred payments, other property)
- Who pays closing costs (the seller may pay the buyer's loan discount points, title policy premium, or other costs. The buyer may pay the seller's brokerage commission)
- Terms of financing, if the seller provides the loan (amount, interest rate, term of loan)
- Guarantees (the seller may guarantee a minimum rental income)
- Timing of closing (the buyer may wish to delay the closing to allow time to arrange financing or sign up tenants)
- Contingencies (sale subject to financing or sale of another property)

It is important to recognize that the total cost of the transaction is what counts, not merely the stated price. If you are willing to meet the seller's price, you may be able to get concessions on other items that may be more important. For example, the seller may be willing to finance the sale by lending a substantial amount of the cost. The interest rate and repayment terms then become crucial issues. Getting a lower interest rate on a long-term loan, even if only 1 percent lower, can be equivalent to a property price reduction of up to 10 percent.

When negotiating, you shouldn't feel that you are trying to take advantage of the other party. Recognize that offers contain margins for bargaining and your objective is to get the best deal possible. At the same time, you must be realistic in your demands and be willing to compromise if you really want to close the deal.

46

SELLER FINANCING AND PRICE

Sometimes a piece of real estate is offered with financing. In many cases, the terms are better than those possible from outside lenders, so this type of financing can be very advantageous. Not only does it make financing the purchase easier, but the terms offer considerable savings. Indeed, the financing may make the purchase a bargain even if you pay market value for the property.

Therefore, you should take the provision of favorable financing terms into consideration when determining your reservation price. Although terms on a loan and a lump sum price appear to be two different things, there are techniques for converting one to the other for comparison. In finance jargon, this is called "cash equivalence," and it is a valuable tool for finding the real price paid for a property.

In essence, when you buy a property with seller financing, you are buying two items: real property and financing terms. If the terms of the loan are the same as those on other loans in the market, the terms have no special value. What makes them valuable are the monthly savings you may enjoy during the financing period. These savings are the difference between what you would have paid with market financing and what you are actually paying as a result of the seller financing. You can convert these monthly savings into a lump sum value estimate of the savings today, called a "present value." Doing so requires a technique called "discounting," which simply means that a $1 dollar in savings today is more valuable than a $1 in savings later because of potential interest earnings. Consider it a discount on the price of the property. You can base the discount on the full loan term or a shorter period if you anticipate a sale or refinancing before the loan is fully paid off.

An accurate estimate of cash equivalence involves some rather detailed calculations that require a financial calculator or set of tables. However, in most cases, you will not need to be highly precise in your analysis. A general idea of the magnitude of savings possible is enough to reflect it in your reservation price. The table below has been worked out as an aid in the process.

The table is based on a market rate of interest of 10 percent. If the actual rate is more or less, it will not make a big difference. The numbers in the table are the approximate percent of discount from the asking price represented by the financing terms. In other words, you can afford to add that much more to the asking price in exchange for the financing terms. The rows refer to the percentage of the price that can be financed. The columns refer to how many percentage points the interest rate is below the market rate. Each column is divided into loans of 25 and 20 years.

For example, say a home is offered for $100,000. The seller will provide a loan of $75,000 (75 percent of the price) for 20 years at an interest rate one percentage point below the market. Looking at the 75 percent row and the column under one percentage point and 20 years, we find the discount to be 6 percent. A price of $106,000 (or 6 percent higher) with the financing terms is equivalent to paying $100,000 and financing with a market-rate loan.

The body of the table shows the increase in price to compensate for a below-market interest rate.

Percentage Points Below Market Interest Rate

| Loan/ | One Percent | | Two Percent | | Three Percent | |
Price	25 yrs	20 yrs	25 yrs	20 yrs	25 yrs	20 yrs
100%	9	8	21	17	34	28
75%	7	6	15	13	25	21
50%	5	4	10	9	17	14

47

CONDOMINIUM CONSIDERATIONS

A large part of the foreclosure market is in condominiums. There are hundreds of thousands of "condo slaves," people who bought condos at high prices and high interest rates who can't afford to absorb a loss from a sale and don't have the cash to refinance them. For example, a person may have bought a condo for $100,000 with a $90,000 loan at 15 percent. The property is now worth $60,000, and interest rates in the market are 7 percent. However, a new lender will only lend 80 percent of current value ($48,000), which means that the present owner must present $32,000 in cash to reduce the current loan to $48,000 before it can be refinanced at 7 percent or sold at market value. This may be impossible, so the present owner continues the existing terms, absorbing the loss in high payments as a preference to abandonment with a loss in credit rating.

There are opportunities to buy condos at distressed prices. Look carefully at the situation before buying, especially at resale opportunities. All real estate, especially condos, can be like a mousetrap—easy to get into, hard to get out of. There are also some lifestyle considerations.

The biggest difference between living in a single-family, detached home and a condo or co-op is the close proximity of your neighbors. When you live in a detached home, you have a buffer of lawn and maybe a fence between you and your neighbor. In a condo or co-op, this division is often no more than a common wall. In addition, once you are outside your unit, you are sharing space with the other residents. One of the most important considerations in buying a condo or co-op is deciding whether this type of living arrangement is suitable for you and your family.

Condo/co-op living does have certain advantages. Among them are:

Cost. Multi-family housing uses less land and is often more economical to build because of common structural components and other design features. Therefore, these units are generally less expensive than detached homes of similar size and quality. (Of course, condo/co-ops can be very expensive housing when placed in exclusive locations, such as Park Avenue in New York.) Lower priced units are good starter homes for first-time home buyers. Lower prices mean smaller loan amounts, making it easier for young families to qualify for a mortgage. Attached units may be less expensive to heat and cool because of the insulating effect of neighboring units.

Location. Because they take less land per unit, condo/co-ops can be developed on high-cost land within major cities. This appeals to people who like being closer to downtown business and entertainment centers. On the other hand, these locations may not be as residential in character as single-family neighborhoods. This is a judgment you must make based on your desired lifestyle.

Low maintenance. A big attraction for some condo/co-op residents is the freedom from many of the routine household tasks. Things like lawn maintenance and outside repairs are generally the responsibility of the association or board. You pay for these services through your monthly fee, but this is often cheaper than contracting independently for these services.

Lifestyle. Some complexes are specifically designed to promote certain lifestyles. There may be organized social functions for young single adults. Older single people may like the security of having neighbors close by. Elaborate common area facilities may be conducive to entertaining. However, most complexes are not amenable to residents with small children, pets, or those who like gardening.

There are also disadvantages to living in attached housing. This is why some people would not be happy living in a condo or co-op. If the following concerns bother you, you should consider an alternative to buying a condo/co-op.

Privacy. This is probably the biggest objection many people have to condos and co-ops. Good design can minimize this problem. Soundproofing in common walls and ceilings, private entryways (often associated with townhouse designs), and private patios and decks can reduce the intrusion of your neighbors. However, attached housing frequently involves some loss of freedom.

Control. Much of what you do in your home is determined by the by-laws of the condo/co-op and majority rule of the owners association or corporation. If you cherish the independence that homeownership entails, you may not want to own a condo or co-op.

Status. In many parts of the United States, condos and co-ops are indistinguishable from rental apartments. Therefore, you may find that much of the status advantage normally attached to homeownership is lost when you own a condo or co-op. In some areas, mortgage financing for these units has been a problem. Lenders either are unfamiliar with condo/co-op ownership or feel that the units are not as marketable as, and therefore less valuable collateral than, detached homes. By contrast, a Manhattan condo or cooperative is fashionable.

Appreciation. Markets for condos have been less stable than those for detached homes. In some areas, builders have badly overestimated the market, and a surplus of condos exist. Then, too, if demand for condos increases, rental apartments can be converted quickly to increase the supply. This means your unit may not increase in value as rapidly as other types of housing.

Resale restrictions. For co-ops, the authority of the board to screen prospective tenants may complicate your ability to sell your unit for the best price. By contrast, condo sales may generally be effected without neighbors' approval.

(For more information, see Barron's *Keys to Purchasing a Condo or a Co-op.*)

48

INVESTMENT ANALYSIS

Investment analysis is deciding if a particular investment opportunity is right for you. This involves knowing what you want and being able to figure out which investment is likely to satisfy your goals. This requires several steps. First, you must determine your investment objectives and translate them into criteria. These criteria allow you to reject inappropriate investments and pick the best of those that are appropriate. Next, decide on the type of investment: real estate, stocks, bonds, precious metals, etc. This choice depends on current asset prices and how you expect them to change in the future. It also depends on how your present investment portfolio is composed and how much diversification you need.

After you have some idea of what you want, the next step is to screen the available opportunities to eliminate those that don't fit your criteria. You may seek an expert to help you decide what to consider. When you have a set of investment alternatives that generally fit your requirements, try to decide on the best one. This consists of projecting how the investment is likely to perform, considering the chance that something will go wrong, and comparing the projected return to those offered by other investment opportunities.

There are several ways to approach investment analysis for real estate. Some investors like to review all information. Others prefer to play a hunch as to what will work. Some like detailed projections. Others base their decision on inspection of the property and surrounding area. Some try to find properties that are undervalued in the market. Others emphasize negotiation to make a profitable deal. Many investors take a short-term perspective and look only at current performance. Others take a long-term viewpoint and look for value appreciation.

Regardless of the approach, you need a projection of investment return to make a decision. Since the return from real estate investments depends on future rent, operating expenses, financing, and tax considerations, by estimating these you can estimate how the property will perform. Projections may be the focus of the decision or may supplement other sources of information. The important thing to remember is that projections are only as good as the assumptions used to make them. Assuming rapid increases in rental rates and unrealistic appreciation rates can make any investment look good. It is best to take a conservative approach to the projection and let speculation about possible improved perfor mance be a separate factor in the decision.

Short-term analysis can be used to screen properties. The following indicators may be calculated quickly with a few bits of information that are based on current performance:

Gross rent multiplier. This is the total gross rent divided by the price of the property. The lower the num ber, the less you are paying for the gross income. For example, a property that sells for $100,000 and rents for $1,000 per month has a multiplier of 100. If all other things were equal (operating costs, future value expectations) that would be a bargain compared to a property that costs 125 times the monthly rent.

Overall rate of return or capitalization rate. This is the net operating income (rent less operating expenses) divided by the value of the property. This measure is preferred to the gross rent multiplier because it accounts for operating expenses. Also, it offers a percentage rate, which is a customary way to express rate of return. For example, if a property rents for $1,000 per month and the owner is responsible for taxes and insurance that total $250 per month, the amount left is $750 per month.

For 12 months that is $9,000, or a 9 percent return on a $100,000 investment, the overall rate of return. You should also provide a vacancy and collection allowance and detail all operating costs that the owner will bear. This example was kept simple by just indicating some likely expenses.

Cash-on-cash return or equity dividend rate. This is the cash flow divided by the required equity investment, and is especially useful when you know how the property will be financed. You may use before-tax or after-tax cash flow. If after-tax cash flow is used, you should adjust the returns on alternative types of investment for taxes to make a meaningful comparison.

Long-term analysis requires more information and assumptions because you are projecting several years into the future. If you are considering a property whose value is likely to increase or decrease in the near future, of if inflation is significant, long-term analysis is probably worthwhile.

Potential investors need to be reminded that most real estate is not a passive investment. Typically, the owner must manage the property or go to the effort of finding a property manager and giving instructions regarding management policies. The owner must then keep the manager accountable for property management, including investment results. Details of investment criteria and further explanation of real estate investment considerations are offered in Barron's *Keys to Investing in Real Estate.*

49

APPRAISALS

An appraisal is an expert opinion of value. An expert is someone with the competence and experience to do the type of analysis required. You can get opinions of value from sales agents, the owner, the tenant, or anyone familiar with the property. However, these opinions may not be very useful and probably won't be convincing as evidence of value. Usually, an appraisal expert has attained some type of designation through formal study and examination by a recognized body.

For example, the MAI and SRA designations are awarded by the Appraisal Institute to those who pass certain tests, prepare detailed sample reports called demonstrations, and complete years of appraisal experience. Other highly credible organizations that award appraisal designations include the National Society of Real Estate Appraisers, the American Society of Appraisers, the International Association of Assessing Officers, and the National Association of Independent Fee Appraisers. Designations from these associations assure that the appraiser understands the principles of appraisal and subscribes to a code of professional ethics. All states are now required to license appraisers of real property.

An opinion is a judgment supported by facts and logical analysis. The appraiser considers all available information that reflects on the value of the property. He or she follows a logical process to arrive at the opinion. The result is not merely a guess but a careful reading of the facts in the case. A good appraiser avoids interjecting personal bias into the opinion and tries to figure out how the market views the property.

Value should be qualified as well. There are different

types of value. The majority of appraisals seek to find *market value*. This is what the property is worth to typical purchasers in a normal market. It is used as a standard in many applications. If you are interested in what the property is worth under your personal circumstances, an appraisal can be made for *investment value*. An appraiser should be able to give an opinion of value under any conditions, as long as they are spelled out at the outset.

Most appraisals are used for factual support. Lenders use them to show that a property is worth enough to serve as collateral for a loan. Appraisals may be used in condemnation cases to award compensation. They can be used to challenge property tax assessments or to back up an income tax return. They may be used in settling an estate.

Appraisals may be used as decision tools as well. You can get an appraisal to help decide how much to offer. They may serve to assist banks when trying to manage repossessed properties or to work out a troubled project.

An appraisal does not determine the market price—it is supposed to follow or reflect what is happening in the market. However, if the property under contract has been priced above the appraised value, a lender may not provide the necessary loan. Instead, the lender may suggest that the price be renegotiated to a lower amount (or force the buyer to pay the difference in cash). In doing so, the appraisal may in fact determine the market price, contradicting its purpose as stated above.

GLOSSARY

Many of the following terms were adapted from the *Real Estate Handbook* or the *Dictionary of Real Estate Terms*, copyright Barron's Educational Series, Inc., Hauppauge, New York.

Absolute auction All properties are sold to the highest bidder; the seller has no reservation prices.

Acceleration Causing the full amount of a loan to be due upon default of certain provisions.

Acceptance Agreeing to take an offer; the acceptance of an offer constitutes a contract.

Acre Measure of land containing 43,560 square feet.

Ad valorem tax Tax based on the value of the property.

Addendum An attachment to a contract, often to describe required inspections or financing terms.

Adjustable-rate mortgage (ARM) Loan where the interest rate fluctuates according to another rate, as when the mortgage rate is adjusted annually based on the one-year Treasury bill rate, plus a 2 percent margin.

Agency Legal relationship between a principal and agent arising from a contract in which the principal engages the agent to perform certain acts on the principal's behalf.

Agent One who undertakes to transact some business or to manage some affair for another, with the authority of the latter.

Agreement of sale Written agreement between buyer and seller to transfer real estate at a future date. Includes all the conditions required for a sale.

Amortization Gradual process of reducing a debt in a systematic manner.

Appraisal An expert's opinion on the value of property arrived at with careful consideration of all available and relevant data.

Appreciation Increase in the value of property.

As is Present condition of property. The "as is" clause is likely to warn of a defect.

Assessed value Value against which a property tax is imposed. The assessed value is often lower than the market value due to state law, conservative tax district appraisals, and infrequent appraisals.

Assignment Method by which a right or contract is transferred from one person to another.

Assumable mortgage Loan that can be transferred to another party. The transferee assumes the debt, but the original borrower is not released from the debt without a novation.

Auction An announced event whereby property is sold to the highest bidder. See *Absolute auction, Dutch auction.*

Balloon mortgage Loan having a large final payment.

Balloon payment Large final payment on a debt.

Bid The amount one offers to pay for real estate.

Bill of sale Document used to transfer personal property. Often used in conjunction with a real estate transaction where appliances or furniture are sold also.

Binder Brief agreement, accompanied by a deposit, showing intent to follow with a formal contract.

Bridge loan Mortgage financing between the termination of one loan and the beginning of another.

Broker One who is licensed by a state to act for property owners in real estate transactions, within the scope of state law.

Building codes Regulations established by local governments describing the minimum structural requirements for buildings; includes foundation, roofing, plumbing, electrical, and other specifications for safety and sanitation.

Cap Maximum rate of change of the interest rate on an adjustable-rate mortgage. The mortgage may have an annual or lifetime ceiling.

Capital gain Gain on the sale of a capital asset. If long-term (generally over six months), capital gains are favorably taxed.

Caveat emptor "Let the buyer beware." An expression once used in real estate to put the burden of an undisclosed defect on the buyer. This concept has been eroded in most states.

Chattels Personal property.

Clear title Title that connotes ownership free from clouds; marketable title.

Closing Date when buyer and seller exchange money for property.

Closing costs Various fees and expenses payable by the seller and buyer at the time of a real estate closing (also termed *Transaction costs*). Included are brokerage commissions, discount points, title insurance and examination, deed recording fees, and appraisal fees.

Closing statement Accounting of funds from a real estate sale, made to both the seller and the buyer separately. Most states require the broker to furnish accurate closing statements to all parties to the transaction.

Cloud on title Outstanding claim or encumbrance that, if valid, would affect or impair the owner's title. Compare *Clear title.*

Commission 1. Amount earned by a real estate broker for his services. 2. Official state agency that enforces real estate licensing laws.

Commitment letter Written pledge or promise; a firm agreement, often used to describe the terms of a mortgage loan that is being offered.

Common elements In a condominium, those portions of the property not owned individually by unit owners but in which an indivisible interest is held by all unit owners. Generally includes the grounds, parking areas, maintenance areas, recreational facilities, and external structure of the building.

Community property Property accumulated through joint efforts of husband and wife and owned by them in equal shares. This doctrine of ownership now exists in Arizona, California, Idaho, Louisiana, Nevada, New Mexico, Texas, and Washington State.

Comparables Properties that are similar to the one being sold or appraised. Used in the market approach to appraisal.

Competitive market analysis An estimate of what a property might bring based on the sale or offering of similar properties, usually by a real estate salesperson. Contrast *Appraisal.*

Conditional offer One that requires certain condition(s) to be fulfilled, such as rezoning of the property or the buyer's need to sell another property, before the contract is binding.

Conditional sales contract Written agreement for the sale of property stating that the seller retains title until the conditions of the contract have been fulfilled. See *Contract for deed.*

Condominium System of ownership of individual units in a multi-unit structure, combined with joint ownership of commonly used property (sidewalks, hallways, stairs, etc.). See *Common elements*.

Consideration Anything of value given to induce entering into a contract; it may be money, personal services, or love and affection.

Contingency Condition that must be satisfied before the party to a contract must purchase or sell. For example, financing is the most frequent contingency. A buyer who cannot arrange an appropriate loan need not complete the transaction and should receive a refund of the earnest money.

Contract Agreement between competent parties to do or not to do certain things for a consideration. Common real estate contracts are contract of sale, contract for deed, mortgage, lease, listing, deed.

Contract for deed Real estate installment sales arrangement whereby the buyer may use, occupy, and enjoy land, but no deed is given by the seller (so no title passes) until all or a specified part of the sale price has been paid. Same as *Land contract, Installment land contract, Conditional sales contract*.

Contract of sale Same as *Agreement of sale*.

Conventional loan, mortgage 1. Mortgage loan other than one guaranteed by the Veterans Administration or insured by the Federal Housing Administration. See *VA loan, FHA loan*. 2. Fixed-rate, fixed-term mortgage loan.

Cooperative Type of corporate ownership of real property whereby stockholders of the corporation are entitled to use a certain dwelling unit or other units of space. Special income tax laws allow the tenant stockholders to deduct interest and property taxes paid by the corporation.

Curtesy Right of a husband to all or part of his deceased wife's realty regardless of the provisions of her will. Exists in only a few states.

Deed Written document, properly signed and delivered, that conveys title to real property. See *General warranty deed, Quitclaim deed, Special warranty deed*.

Deed of trust Instrument used in many states in lieu of a mortgage. Legal title to the property is vested in one or more trustees to secure the repayment of the loan.

Deed restriction Clause in a deed that limits the use of land.

Default Failure to fulfill an obligation or promise or to perform specified acts.

Deficiency judgment Court order stating that the borrower still owes money when the security for a loan does not entirely satisfy a defaulted debt.

Department of Housing and Urban Development (HUD) U.S. government agency established to implement certain federal housing and community development programs.

Depreciation 1. In accounting, allocating the cost of an asset over its estimated useful life. 2. In appraisal, a charge against the reproduction cost (new) of an asset for the estimated wear and obsolescence. Depreciation may be physical, functional, or economic.

Discount points Amounts paid to the lender (often by the seller) at the time of origination of a loan, to account for the difference between the market interest rate and the lower face rate of the note.

Dower Under common law, the legal right of a wife or child to part of a deceased husband or father's property. Compare *Curtesy*.

Down payment Amount one pays for property in addition to the debt incurred.

Due-on-sale clause Provision in a mortgage that states that the loan is due upon the sale of the property.

Dutch auction The price is gradually lowered until a purchase occurs.

Earnest money Deposit made before closing by a purchaser of real estate to evidence good faith.

Easement Right, privilege, or interest that one party has in the land of another. The most common easements are for utility lines.

Encroachment Building, a part of a building, or an obstruction that physically intrudes upon, overlaps, or trespasses upon the property of another.

Encumbrance Any right to or interest in land that affects its value. Includes outstanding mortgage loans, unpaid taxes, easements, and deed restrictions.

Equity Interest or value that the owner has in real estate over and above the liens against it.

Equity loan Usually a second mortgage whereby the property owner borrows against the house, based on the value of equity built up by appreciation.

135

Equity of redemption The right of a borrower to regain property generally after default, before foreclosure.

Escrow Agreement between two or more parties providing that certain instruments or property be placed with a third party for safekeeping, pending the fulfillment or performance of some act or condition.

Et ux. Abbreviation of the Latin *et uxor*, which means "and wife."

Exclusive agency listing Employment contract giving only one broker, for a specified time, the right to sell the property and also allowing the owner alone to sell the property without paying a commission.

Exclusive right to sell listing Employment contract giving the broker the right to collect a commission if the property is sold by anyone, including the owner, during the term of the agreement. See *Multiple listing service*.

Execute To sign a contract; sometimes, to perform a contract fully.

Fair market value A term generally used in property tax and condemnation legislation, meaning the market value of a property.

Fannie Mae See *Federal National Mortgage Association*.

Federal Fair Housing Law Federal law that forbids discrimination on the basis of race, color, sex, religion, or national origin in the selling or renting of homes and apartments.

Federal Housing Administration (FHA) Agency within the United States Department of Housing and Urban Development that administers many loan programs, loan guarantee programs, and loan insurance programs designed to make more housing available.

Federal National Mortgage Association (FNMA) corporation that specializes in buying mortgage loans, mostly from mortgage bankers. It adds liquidity to the mortgage market. Nicknamed Fannie Mae, FNMA is owned by its stockholders, who elect ten of its board of directors. The United States president appoints the other five directors.

Fee simple or fee absolute Absolute ownership of real property; the owner is entitled to the entire property with unconditional power of disposition during his life, and it descends to his heirs and legal representatives upon his death intestate.

FHA loan Mortgage loan insured by the FHA.

First mortgage Mortgage that has priority as a lien over all other mortgages. In cases of foreclosure, the first mortgage will be satisfied before other mortgages.

Fixed-rate mortgage Loan on which the interest rate does not change over the entire term of the loan.

Fixtures Personal property attached to the land or improvements so as to become part of the real estate.

Foreclosure Termination of all rights of a mortgagor or the grantee in the property covered by the mortgage.

General warranty deed Deed in which the grantor agrees to protect the grantee against any other claim to title to the property and provides other promises.

Graduated-payment mortgage (GPM) Loan requiring lower payments in early years than in later years. Payments increase in steps each year until the installments are sufficient to amortize the loan.

Grantee Party to whom the title to real property is conveyed; the buyer.

Grantor Anyone who gives a deed.

Gross rent multiplier (GRM) Sales price divided by the rental rate.

Growing equity mortgage (GEM) Mortgage loan in which the payment is increased by a specific amount each year, with the additional payment amount applied to principal retirement. As a result of the added principal retirement, the maturity of the loan is significantly shorter than a comparable level-payment mortgage.

Hazard insurance A form of insurance that protects against certain risks, such as fires and storms.

Homeowners' association Organization of the homeowners in a particular subdivision, planned unit development, or condominium; generally for the purpose of enforcing deed restrictions or managing the common elements of the development.

Homeowner's policy Insurance policy designed especially for homeowners. Usually protects the owner from losses caused by most common disasters, theft, and liability. Coverage and costs vary widely.

HUD Department of Housing and Urban Development.
HUD home One that was foreclosed and offered for sale by HUD.

Inside lot In a subdivision, a lot surrounded on each side by other lots, as opposed to a corner lot, which has road frontage on at least two sides.

Joint tenancy Ownership of real estate by two or more persons, each of whom has an undivided interest with the right of survivorship.

Junior mortgage Loan whose claim against the property will be satisfied only after prior mortgages have been repaid. See *First mortgage*.

Land contract Same as *Contract for deed*.

Lien Charge against property making it security for the payment of a debt, judgment, mortgage, or taxes; it is a type of encumbrance. A specific lien is against certain property only. A general lien is against all the property owned by the debtor.

List To give or obtain a listing.

Listing 1. Written engagement contract between a principal and an agent, authorizing the agent to perform services for the principal involving the latter's property. 2. Record of property for sale by a broker who has been authorized by the owner to sell. 3. Property so listed.

Listing agreement, listing contract Same as *Listing* (1).

Loan-to-value ratio (LTV) Amount borrowed as a percentage of the cost or value of the property purchased.

Lot and block number Method of locating a parcel of land. The description refers to a map of a subdivision that numbers each lot and block.

Market value Most probable selling price. Also, theoretical highest price a buyer, willing but not compelled to buy, would pay, and the lowest price a seller, willing but not compelled to sell, would accept.

Mechanic's lien Lien given by law upon a building or other improvement upon land, and upon the land itself, as security for the payment for labor done and materials furnished for improvement.

Mortgage Written instrument that creates a lien upon real estate as security for the payment of a specified debt.

Mortgagee One who holds a lien on property or title to property, as security for a debt; the lender.

Mortgagor One who pledges property as security for a loan; the borrower.

Mortgage banker One who originates, sells, and services mortgage loans. Most loans are insured or guaranteed by a government agency or private mortgage insurer.

Mortgage insurance Protection for the lender in the event of default, usually covering 10 to 20 percent of the amount borrowed.

Multiple listing service (MLS) Association of real estate brokers that agrees to share listings with one another. The listing broker and the selling broker share the commission. The MLS usually distributes a book with all listings to its members, updating the book frequently. Prospective buyers benefit from the ability to select from among many homes listed by any member broker.

National Association of Real Estate Brokers (NAREB) Organization of minority real estate salespersons and brokers who are called *Realtists®*.

National Association of Realtors® (NAR) Organization of *Realtors®*, devoted to encouraging professionalism in real estate activities. There are over 600,000 members of NAR, 50 state associations, and several affiliates.

Negative amortization Increase in the outstanding balance of a loan resulting from the failure of periodic debt service payments to cover required interest charged on the loan.

Net listing Listing in which the broker's commission is the excess of the sales price over an agreed-upon (net) price to the seller; illegal in some states.

Notary public Officer who is authorized to take acknowledgments to certain types of documents, such as deeds, contracts, and mortgages, and before whom affidavits may be sworn.

Novation Agreement whereby a lender substitutes one party to a contract for another, releasing the original party from any obligation.

Reservation price A mental note of the minimum a seller will accept; the maximum a buyer will pay.

Sales contract Same as *Contract of sale*.

Sealed bids Offers submitted in a closed envelope so that other bidders do not see what others are willing to pay.

Secondary mortgage market The "marketplace" where existing mortgages, mostly first mortgages on homes, are traded.

Self-amortizing mortgage Loan that will retire itself through regular principal and interest payments. Contrast with *Balloon mortgage*.

Sellers' market Economic conditions that favor sellers, reflecting rising prices and market activity.

Settlement Same as *Closing*.

Special assessment Assessment made against a property to pay for a public improvement by which the assessed property is supposed to be especially benefited.

Special warranty deed Deed in which the grantor limits the title warranty given to the grantee to anyone claiming by, from, through, or under him, the grantor. The grantor does not warrant against title defects arising from conditions that existed before he owned the property. Often this type of deed is quite satisfactory. For example, a buyer in a foreclosure sale will receive a sheriff's deed, which is a special warranty against claims arising prior to foreclosure.

Specific performance Legal action in which the court requires a party to a contract to perform the terms of the contract when he has refused to fulfill his obligations. Used in real estate, since each parcel of land is unique.

Statutory According to statutes; pertaining to written laws.

Statutory redemption The right of a borrower to regain property that was foreclosed, according to written law.

Subcontractor One who performs services under contract to a general contractor.

Subdivision Tract of land divided into lots or plots suitable for home-building purposes. Some states and localities require that a subdivision plot be recorded.

Subject to mortgage Arrangement whereby a buyer takes title to mortgaged real property but is not personally responsible for the payment of any portion of the amount due. The buyer must make payments in order to keep the property; however, if he fails to do so, only his equity in that property is lost.

142

Survey Process by which a parcel of land is measured and its area ascertained; also, the blueprint showing the measurements, boundaries, and area.

Sweat equity Value added to a property due to improvements as a result of work performed personally by the owner.

Term amortization For a loan, the period of time during which principal and interest payments must be made; generally, the time needed to amortize the loan fully.

Terms Provisions in a contract; interest rate and payment requirements of a loan.

Title Evidence that the owner of land is in lawful possession thereof; evidence of ownership.

Title insurance Insurance policy that protects the holder from loss sustained by defects in the title.

Title search Examination of the public records to determine the ownership and encumbrances affecting real property.

Veterans Administration (VA) Government agency that provides certain services to discharged servicemen.

VA loan (mortgage) Loan that is guaranteed by the Veterans Administration. Honorably discharged servicemen with 90 days service in time of war or 180 days in time of peace (90 days during Desert Storm) or 6 years active service in federal or state reserves are eligible.

Vendee Buyer.

Vendor Seller.

Warranty deed Title to real estate in which the grantor guarantees title. Usually protects against other claimants, liens, or encumbrances and offers good title.

Zoning ordinance Act of city, county, or other authorities specifying the type of use to which property may be put in specific areas. Examples: residential, commercial, industrial.

CHECKLIST

A good checklist is a useful device to try to ensure that nothing has been overlooked. Although a perfect home has yet to be built, a checklist may help determine whether a house has so many negatives that it is unsuitable for you, or has a "fatal flaw"—something you wouldn't want to own at any price. Use the list to help jog your memory about each feature.

General Checklist

Address
Date shown
Shown by
Owner's name
Phone number
Reason for selling
Availability or Urgency of sale
Age
Price
Special financing
    Assumption, seller
Loan status:
    Delinquent
    Default
    Foreclosed by:
    Local institution
    HUD
    VA
    Private mortgage insurer
Relocation company ownership
Taxes
Builder
Style, stories, or levels
Construction quality
Comments

Location Characteristics

	Superior	Average	Inferior

School district
   Elementary
   Junior high
   High
   Parochial
Fire and police protection
Transportation
Medical facilities
Shopping
Recreational
Religious facilities
Neighborhood
Subdivision
Homeowner association
View
Crime statistics in neighborhood
Registry of sexual offenders living in area

Interior Arrangements

	Superior	Average	Inferior

Number of bedrooms
   Closet(s) size, shelving
Number of bathrooms
   Size, fixtures, floor
Living room
Family room
Laundry/utility room
Floor plan
Floor coverings
Window treatments
Built-in cabinets
Paint
Wallpaper
Fireplace
Basement
Additional Comments

House Exterior—Quality or Condition

	Superior	Average	Inferior
Roof			
Façade			
Windows			
Drainage			
Paint			
Garage (size, attached)			
Attic			
Storage			
Additional Comments			

Lot

	Superior	Average	Inferior
Size, shape			
Fence			
Shrubbery			
Trees			
Lawn			
Sprinklers			
Swimming pool			
Patio			
Driveway			
Traffic			
Zoning			
Flood plain			
Environmental hazards			
Additional Comments			

Servicing

	Superior	Average	Inferior
Waste (sewer, septic			
Heating			
Air conditioning			
Insulation			
Ceiling			
Walls			
Weather-stripping			
Storm windows, doors			
Wiring			
Plumbing			
Appliances			
Additional Comments			

Negotiating

Asking price
Probable price
Financing
Points
Closing costs
   Legal
   Recording
   Appraisal
Inspections
   Inside
   Outside
   Pests
Contingencies
   Sale of old house
   Mortgage approval
   Mortgage terms
Additional Comments

Financing

Existing financing
    Assumability
    Lender(s), account numbers, phone numbers
    Unpaid balance(s), interest rate, remaining term, balloons
    Transfer fees
    Prepayment penalty
New Financing
Lender name   **Type**
and phone   **(Fixed, Adj) Rate L-T-V Term Points**
    Fees Lock-in Other

Legal Considerations

Deed type
Homestead exemption
Spouse's name
Ownership form
    (joint tenancy, community property)
Title policy or abstract
Exceptions on title policy
Attorney's opinion of title
Additional Comments

PAYMENT TABLES

To calculate monthly payment requirements from tables on following pages:

1. Find intersection of Contract Interest Rate with Term (Years).
2. Multiply amount in table by thousands borrowed to result in monthly principal and interest payment.
3. Add estimated taxes and insurance (not shown on table).

Example: Find the monthly payment on a $90,000 loan for 25 years at 9½ percent interest.
Step 1.   8.74 (read from table).
Step 2.   Multiply by 90.
            Result $786.60 is the monthly principal and interest payment.
Step 3.   Add monthly tax and insurance requirement.

Monthly Principal and Interest Payments
per $1,000 of Principal

Term (Years)	Contract Interest Rate (%) 6.00	6.25	6.50	6.75
1	86.07	86.18	86.30	86.41
2	44.32	44.43	44.55	44.66
3	30.42	30.54	30.65	30.76
4	23.49	23.60	23.71	23.83
5	19.33	19.45	19.57	19.68
6	16.57	16.69	16.81	16.93
7	14.61	14.73	14.85	14.97
8	13.14	13.26	13.39	13.51
9	12.01	12.13	12.25	12.38
10	11.10	11.23	11.35	11.48
11	10.37	10.49	10.62	10.75
12	9.76	9.89	10.02	10.15
13	9.25	9.38	9.51	9.65
14	8.81	8.95	9.08	9.22
15	8.44	8.57	8.71	8.85
16	8.11	8.25	8.39	8.53
17	7.83	7.97	8.11	8.25
18	7.58	7.72	7.87	8.01
19	7.36	7.50	7.65	7.79
20	7.16	7.31	7.46	7.60
21	6.99	7.14	7.28	7.43
22	6.83	6.98	7.13	7.28
23	6.69	6.84	6.99	7.14
24	6.56	6.71	6.87	7.02
25	6.44	6.60	6.75	6.91
26	6.34	6.49	6.65	6.81
27	6.24	6.40	6.56	6.72
28	6.15	6.31	6.47	6.63
29	6.07	6.23	6.39	6.56
30	6.00	6.16	6.32	6.49

Monthly Principal and Interest Payments
per $1,000 of Principal

Term (Years)	Contract Interest Rate (%)			
	7.00	7.25	7.50	7.75
1	86.53	86.64	86.76	86.87
2	44.77	44.89	45.00	45.11
3	30.88	30.99	31.11	31.22
4	23.95	24.06	24.18	24.30
5	19.80	19.92	20.04	20.16
6	17.05	17.17	17.29	17.41
7	15.09	15.22	15.34	15.46
8	13.63	13.76	13.88	14.01
9	12.51	12.63	12.76	12.89
10	11.61	11.74	11.87	12.00
11	10.88	11.02	11.15	11.28
12	10.28	10.42	10.55	10.69
13	9.78	9.92	10.05	10.19
14	9.35	9.49	9.63	9.77
15	8.99	9.13	9.27	9.41
16	8.67	8.81	8.96	9.10
17	8.40	8.54	8.69	8.83
18	8.16	8.30	8.45	8.60
19	7.94	8.09	8.24	8.39
20	7.75	7.90	8.06	8.21
21	7.58	7.74	7.89	8.05
22	7.43	7.59	7.75	7.90
23	7.30	7.46	7.61	7.77
24	7.18	7.34	7.50	7.66
25	7.07	7.23	7.39	7.55
26	6.97	7.13	7.29	7.46
27	6.88	7.04	7.21	7.37
28	6.80	6.96	7.13	7.30
29	6.72	6.89	7.06	7.23
30	6.65	6.82	6.99	7.16

Monthly Principal and Interest Payments
per $1,000 of Principal

Term (Years)	Contract Interest Rate (%)			
	8.00	8.25	8.50	8.75
1	86.99	87.10	87.22	87.34
2	45.23	45.34	45.46	45.57
3	31.34	31.45	31.57	31.68
4	24.41	24.53	24.65	24.77
5	20.28	20.40	20.52	20.64
6	17.53	17.66	17.78	17.90
7	15.59	15.71	15.84	15.96
8	14.14	14.26	14.39	14.52
9	13.02	13.15	13.28	13.41
10	12.13	12.27	12.40	12.53
11	11.42	11.55	11.69	11.82
12	10.82	10.96	11.10	11.24
13	10.33	10.47	10.61	10.75
14	9.91	10.06	10.20	10.34
15	9.56	9.70	9.85	9.99
16	9.25	9.40	9.54	9.69
17	8.98	9.13	9.28	9.43
18	8.75	8.90	9.05	9.21
19	8.55	8.70	8.85	9.01
20	8.36	8.52	8.68	8.84
21	8.20	8.36	8.52	8.68
22	8.06	8.22	8.38	8.55
23	7.93	8.10	8.26	8.43
24	7.82	7.98	8.15	8.32
25	7.72	7.88	8.05	8.22
26	7.63	7.79	7.96	8.13
27	7.54	7.71	7.88	8.06
28	7.47	7.64	7.81	7.99
29	7.40	7.57	7.75	7.92
30	7.34	7.51	7.69	7.87

Monthly Principal and Interest Payments
per $1,000 of Principal

Term (Years)	Contract Interest Rate (%)			
	9.00	9.25	9.50	9.75
1	87.45	87.57	87.68	87.80
2	45.68	45.80	45.91	46.03
3	31.80	31.92	32.03	32.15
4	24.88	25.00	25.12	25.24
5	20.76	20.88	21.00	21.12
6	18.03	18.15	18.27	18.40
7	16.09	16.22	16.34	16.47
8	14.65	14.78	14.91	15.04
9	13.54	13.68	13.81	13.94
10	12.67	12.80	12.94	13.08
11	11.96	12.10	12.24	12.38
12	11.38	11.52	11.66	11.81
13	10.90	11.04	11.19	11.33
14	10.49	10.64	10.78	10.93
15	10.14	10.29	10.44	10.59
16	9.85	10.00	10.15	10.30
17	9.59	9.74	9.90	10.05
18	9.36	9.52	9.68	9.84
19	9.17	9.33	9.49	9.65
20	9.00	9.16	9.32	9.49
21	8.85	9.01	9.17	9.34
22	8.71	8.88	9.04	9.21
23	8.59	8.76	8.93	9.10
24	8.49	8.66	8.83	9.00
25	8.39	8.56	8.74	8.91
26	8.31	8.48	8.66	8.83
27	8.23	8.41	8.58	8.76
28	8.16	8.34	8.52	8.70
29	8.10	8.28	8.46	8.64
30	8.05	8.23	8.41	8.59

Monthly Principal and Interest Payments
per $1,000 of Principal

Term (Years)	Contract Interest Rate (%)			
	10.00	10.25	10.50	10.75
1	87.92	88.03	88.15	88.27
2	46.15	46.26	46.38	46.49
3	32.27	32.38	32.50	32.62
4	25.36	25.48	25.60	25.72
5	21.25	21.37	21.49	21.62
6	18.53	18.65	18.78	18.91
7	16.60	16.73	16.86	16.99
8	15.17	15.31	15.44	15.57
9	14.08	14.21	14.35	14.49
10	13.22	13.35	13.49	13.63
11	12.52	12.66	12.80	12.95
12	11.95	12.10	12.24	12.39
13	11.48	11.63	11.78	11.92
14	11.08	11.23	11.38	11.54
15	10.75	10.90	11.05	11.21
16	10.46	10.62	10.77	10.93
17	10.21	10.37	10.53	10.69
18	10.00	10.16	10.32	10.49
19	9.81	9.98	10.14	10.31
20	9.65	9.82	9.98	10.15
21	9.51	9.68	9.85	10.02
22	9.38	9.55	9.73	9.90
23	9.27	9.44	9.62	9.79
24	9.17	9.35	9.52	9.70
25	9.09	9.26	9.44	9.62
26	9.01	9.19	9.37	9.55
27	8.94	9.12	9.30	9.49
28	8.88	9.06	9.25	9.43
29	8.82	9.01	9.19	9.38
30	8.78	8.96	9.15	9.33

Monthly Principal and Interest Payments
per $1,000 of Principal

Term (Years)	11.00	11.25	11.50	11.75
1	88.38	88.50	88.62	88.73
2	46.61	46.72	46.84	46.96
3	32.74	32.86	32.98	33.10
4	25.85	25.97	26.09	26.21
5	21.74	21.87	21.99	22.12
6	19.03	19.16	19.29	19.42
7	17.12	17.25	17.39	17.52
8	15.71	15.84	15.98	16.12
9	14.63	14.76	14.90	15.04
10	13.77	13.92	14.06	14.20
11	13.09	13.24	13.38	13.53
12	12.54	12.68	12.83	12.98
13	12.08	12.23	12.38	12.53
14	11.69	11.85	12.00	12.16
15	11.37	11.52	11.68	11.84
16	11.09	11.25	11.41	11.57
17	10.85	11.02	11.18	11.35
18	10.65	10.82	10.98	11.15
19	10.47	10.64	10.81	10.98
20	10.32	10.49	10.66	10.84
21	10.19	10.36	10.54	10.71
22	10.07	10.25	10.42	10.60
23	9.97	10.15	10.33	10.51
24	9.88	10.06	10.24	10.42
25	9.80	9.98	10.16	10.35
26	9.73	9.91	10.10	10.28
27	9.67	9.85	10.04	10.23
28	9.61	9.80	9.99	10.18
29	9.57	9.75	9.94	10.13
30	9.52	9.71	9.90	10.09

Monthly Principal and Interest Payments
per $1,000 of Principal

Term	Contract Interest Rate (%)			
(Years)	**12.00**	**12.25**	**12.50**	**12.75**
1	88.85	88.97	89.08	89.20
2	47.07	47.19	47.31	47.42
3	33.21	33.33	33.45	33.57
4	26.33	26.46	26.58	26.70
5	22.24	22.37	22.50	22.63
6	19.55	19.68	19.81	19.94
7	17.65	17.79	17.92	18.06
8	16.25	16.39	16.53	16.67
9	15.18	15.33	15.47	15.61
10	14.35	14.49	14.64	14.78
11	13.68	13.83	13.98	14.13
12	13.13	13.29	13.44	13.59
13	12.69	12.84	13.00	13.15
14	12.31	12.47	12.63	12.79
15	12.00	12.16	12.33	12.49
16	11.74	11.90	12.07	12.23
17	11.51	11.68	11.85	12.02
18	11.32	11.49	11.66	11.83
19	11.15	11.33	11.50	11.67
20	11.01	11.19	11.36	11.54
21	10.89	11.06	11.24	11.42
22	10.78	10.96	11.14	11.32
23	10.69	10.87	11.05	11.23
24	10.60	10.79	10.97	11.16
25	10.53	10.72	10.90	11.09
26	10.47	10.66	10.84	11.03
27	10.41	10.60	10.79	10.98
28	10.37	10.56	10.75	10.94
29	10.32	10.52	10.71	10.90
30	10.29	10.48	10.67	10.87

Monthly Principal and Interest Payments
per $1,000 of Principal

Term (Years)	Contract Interest Rate (%)			
	13.00	**13.25**	**13.50**	**13.75**
1	89.32	89.43	89.55	89.67
2	47.54	47.66	47.78	47.90
3	33.69	33.81	33.94	34.06
4	26.83	26.95	27.08	27.20
5	22.75	22.88	23.01	23.14
6	20.07	20.21	20.34	20.47
7	18.19	18.33	18.46	18.60
8	16.81	16.95	17.09	17.23
9	15.75	15.90	16.04	16.19
10	14.93	15.08	15.23	15.38
11	14.28	14.43	14.58	14.73
12	13.75	13.90	14.06	14.21
13	13.31	13.47	13.63	13.79
14	12.95	13.11	13.28	13.44
15	12.65	12.82	12.98	13.15
16	12.40	12.57	12.74	12.91
17	12.19	12.36	12.53	12.70
18	12.00	12.18	12.35	12.53
19	11.85	12.03	12.20	12.38
20	11.72	11.89	12.07	12.25
21	11.60	11.78	11.96	12.15
22	11.50	11.69	11.87	12.05
23	11.42	11.60	11.79	11 97
24	11.34	11.53	11.72	11.91
25	11.28	11.47	11.66	11.85
26	11.22	11.41	11.60	11.80
27	11.17	11.37	11.56	11.75
28	11.13	11.32	11.52	11.71
29	11.09	11.29	11.48	11.68
30	11.06	11.26	11.45	11.65

SALES OFFICES

HUD

Region I (Boston)
Boston Regional Office
Thomas P. O'Neil, Jr.
Federal Building, Room 375
10 Causeway Street
Boston, MA 02222-1092
(617) 565-5236

Hartford
One Corporate Center, 19th Floor
Hartford, CT 06103-3220
(860) 240-4800

Manchester
Norris Cotton Federal Building
275 Chestnut Street
Manchester, NH 03101-2487
(603) 666-7441

Providence
10 Weybosset Street
Providence, RI 02903
(401) 528-5351

Bangor
202 Harbor Street, Room 101
Bangor, ME 04401
(207) 945-0467

Burlington
Federal Building, Room 244
11 Elmwood Avenue
Post Office Box 879
Burlington, VT 05402-0879
(802) 951-6289

Region II (New York)
New York Regional Office
26 Federal Plaza, Room 3541
New York, NY 10278-0068
(212) 264-6500

Albany
52 Corporate Circle
Albany, NY 12203
(518) 464-4200

Buffalo
Lafayette Court
465 Main Street
Buffalo, NY 14203
(716) 551-5755

Camden
Hudson Building
800 Hudson Square, Second Floor
Camden, NJ 08102-1156
(856) 757-5081

Caribbean
171 Carlos Chardon Avenue,
Suite 301
San Juan, PR 00918-0903
(787) 766-5400

Newark
One Newark Center
13th Floor
Newark, NJ 07102
(973) 622-7900

Region III (Philadelphia)
Philadelphia Regional Office
The Wanamaker Building
100 Penn Square East
Philadelphia, PA 19107-3380
(215) 656-0500

Baltimore
10 South Howard Street
Fifth Floor
Baltimore, MD 21201
(410) 962-2520

Charleston
405 Capitol Street, Suite 708
Charleston, WV 25301-1795
(304) 347-7000

Pittsburgh
339 Sixth Avenue
6th Floor
Pittsburgh, PA 15222-2515
(412) 644-6429

Richmond
3600 Centre
3600 West Broad Street
Richmond, VA 23230
(800) 842-2610

Washington, DC
820 First Street, NE, Suite 450
Washington, DC 20002
(202) 275-9200

Wilmington
824 Market Street, Suite 850
Wilmington, DE 19801-3016
(302) 573-6358

Region IV (Atlanta)
Atlanta Regional Office
Richard B. Russell Federal
Building
75 Spring Street, SW, Suite 600
Atlanta, GA 30303
(404) 331-5136

Birmingham
600 Beacon Parkway West
Suite 300
Birmingham, AL 35209
(205) 290-7630

Columbia
Strom Thurmond Federal Building
1835 Assembly Street, 11th Floor
Columbia, SC 29201
(803) 253-3292

Greensboro
Kroger Building
2306 West Meadowview Road
Greensboro, NC 27407-3707
(336) 547-4000

Jackson
Doctor A. H. McCoy Federal
Building
Room 910
100 West Capital Street
Jackson, MS 39269-1096
(601) 965-4700

Jacksonville
301 West Bay Street, Suite 2200
Jacksonville, FL 32202
(904) 232-2627

Knoxville
John J. Duncan Federal Building
Third Floor
710 Locust Street
Knoxville, TN 37902-2526
(423) 545-4304

Louisville
601 West Broadway
Louisville, KY 40202
(502) 582-5251

Memphis
One Memphis Place, Suite 1200
200 Jefferson Avenue
Memphis, TN 38103-2335
(901) 544-3367

Miami
Brickell Plaza Federal Building
909 SE First Avenue, Room 500
Miami, FL 33131-3028
(305) 536-4456

Nashville
251 Cumberland Bend Drive
Suite 200
Nashville, TN 37228-1803
(615) 736-5213

Orlando
Langley Building, Suite 270
3751 Maguire Boulevard
Orlando, FL 32803
(407) 648-6441

Tampa
Timberlake Federal Office
Building
Suite 700
501 East Polk Street
Tampa, FL 33602-3945
(813) 228-2504

Region V (Chicago)
Chicago Regional Office
Ralph H. Metcalfe Federal
Building
77 West Jackson Boulevard
Chicago, IL 60606
(312) 353-5680

Cincinnati
525 Vine Street, Suite 700
Cincinnati, OH 45202
(513) 684-3451

Cleveland
Renaissance on Playhouse Square
1350 Euclid Avenue, Suite 500
Cleveland, OH 44115-1815
(216) 522-4058

Columbus
200 North High Street, 7th Floor
Columbus, OH 43215
(614) 469-5737

Detroit
Patrick J. McNamera Federal
Building
477 Michigan Avenue, Suite 1700
Detroit, MI 48226
(313) 226-7900

Flint
Room 200
605 North Saginaw Street
Flint, MI 48502
(810) 766-5110

Grand Rapids
50 Louis, NW
Grand Rapids, MI 49503-2648
(616) 456-2100

Indianapolis
151 North Delaware Street
Indianapolis, IN 46204-2526
(317) 226-6303

Milwaukee
Henry S. Reuss Federal Plaza
Suite 1380
310 West Wisconsin Avenue
Milwaukee, WI 53203
(414) 297-3214

Minneapolis-St. Paul
220 Second Street, South
Minneapolis, MN 55401-2195
(612) 370-3000

Region VI (Fort Worth)
Fort Worth Regional Office
1600 Throckmorton
Fort Worth, TX 76102
(817) 978-9000

Albuquerque
625 Silver Avenue SW, Suite 100
Albuquerque, NM 87102-3185
(505) 346-6706

Dallas
525 South Griffin Street
Suite 860
Dallas, TX 75202
(214) 767-8300

Houston
Norfolk Tower, Suite 200
2211 Norfolk
Houston, TX 77098-4096
(713) 313-2274

Little Rock
Suite 900
425 West Capitol
Little Rock, AR 72201
(501) 324-5931

Lubbock
George H. Mahon
Federal Office Building
1205 Texas Avenue, Suite 511
Lubbock, TX 79401
(806) 472-7265

New Orleans
Hale Boggs Federal Building,
Ninth Floor
501 Magazine Street
New Orleans, LA 70130-3099
(504) 589-6570

Oklahoma City
500 West Main Street, Suite 400
Oklahoma, OK 73102
(405) 553-7509

San Antonio
Washington Square
800 Dolorosa
San Antonio, TX 78207-4563
(210) 475-6806

Shreveport
401 Edwards Street, Suite 1510
Shreveport, LA 71101-5513
(318) 676-3385

Tulsa
50 East 15th Street
Tulsa, OK 74119
(918) 581-7168

Region VII (Kansas City)
Kansas City Regional Office
Gateway Tower II
400 State Avenue
Kansas City, KS 66101
(913) 551-5644

Des Moines
Federal Building, Room 239
210 Walnut Street
Des Moines, IA 50309-2155
(515) 284-4512

Omaha
10909 Mill Valley Road
Omaha, NE 68154
(402) 492-3100

St. Louis
1222 Spruce Street
St. Louis, MO 63103-2836
(314) 539-6583

Region VIII (Denver)
Denver Regional Office
633 17th Street
Denver, CO 80202
(303) 672-5440

Casper
100 East B Street
Room 4229
Casper, WY 82601
(307) 261-6250

Fargo
Federal Building
657 2nd Avenue North
Post Office Box 2483
Fargo, ND 58108-2483
(701) 239-5040

Helena
Federal Office Building
Room 340
Drawer 10095
301 South Park
Helena, MT 59626-0095
(406) 441-1300

Salt Lake City
257 East 200 South
Suite 550
Salt Lake City, UT 84111-2048
(801) 524-3574

Sioux Falls
2400 West 49th Street
Suite 1-201
Sioux Falls, SD 57105
(605) 330-4223

Region IX (San Francisco)
San Francisco Regional Office
Phillip Burton Federal Building
and U.S. Courthouse
450 Golden Gate Avenue
San Francisco, CA 94102
(415) 436-6550

Fresno
2135 Fresno Street
Suite 100
Fresno, CA 93721-1718
(559) 487-5033

Honolulu
Prince Jonah Federal Building
300 Ala Moana Boulevard
Honolulu, HI 96813
(808) 522-8185

Las Vegas
333 North Rancho Road
Suite 700
Las Vegas, NV 89106
(702) 388-6500

Los Angeles
AT&T Building
611 West Sixth Street, Suite 800
Los Angeles, CA 90017
(213) 894-8000

Phoenix
400 North Fifth Street
Suite 1600
Phoenix, AZ 85004
(602) 379-4461

Reno
1050 Bible Way
Post Office Box 4700
Reno, NV 89505-4700
(702) 784-5356

Sacramento
925 L Street
Sacramento, CA 95814
(916) 498-5220

San Diego
Mission City Corporate Center
2365 Northside Drive, Suite 300
San Diego, CA 92108-2712
(619) 557-5305

Santa Ana
1600 North Broadway
Suite 100
Santa Ana, CA 92706-3927
(888) 827-5605

Tucson
33 North Stone Avenue
Suite 700
Tucson, AZ 85701
(520) 670-6000

Region X (Seattle)
Seattle Regional Office
Seattle Federal Office Building
909 1st Avenue, Suite 200
Seattle, WA 98104
(206) 220-5104

Anchorage
University Plaza Building
949 East 36th Avenue, Suite 401
Anchorage, AK 99508-4399
(907) 271-4663

Boise
Plaza IV, Suite 220
800 Park Boulevard
Boise, ID 83712
(208) 334-1990

Portland
400 Southwest Sixth Avenue
Suite 700
Portland, OR 97204
(503) 326-2561

Spokane
West 920 Riverside Avenue
Spokane, WA 99201-1075
(509) 353-0674

VA
(Note: National toll-free number
for information (800) 827-1000.)
(E-mail: You can E-mail regional
offices directly from
http://www.vba.va.gov/
BENEFITS/address.htm.)

Alabama
345 Perry Hill Road
Montgomery, AL 36109

Alaska
2925 Debarr Road
Anchorage, AK 99508

Arizona
3225 North Central Avenue
Phoenix, AZ 85012

Arkansas
Post Office Box 1280, Fort Roots
North Little Rock, AR 72115

California
Federal Building
11000 Wilshire Boulevard
Los Angeles, CA 90024

1301 Clay Street
Room 1270 North
Oakland, CA 94612

8810 Rio San Diego Drive
San Diego, CA 92108
(619) 400-5340

Colorado
155 Van Gordon
Box 25126
Denver, CO 80225

Connecticut
450 Main Street
Hartford, CT 06103

Delaware
1601 Kirkwood Highway
Wilmington, DE 19805

District of Columbia
1120 Vermont Avenue, NW
Washington, DC 20421

Florida
9500 Bay Pines Boulevard
Bay Pines, FL 33708

Georgia
730 Peachtree Street, NE
Atlanta, GA 30365

Hawaii
Post Office Box 50188
Honolulu, HI 96850

Idaho
805 West Franklin Street
Boise, ID 83702

Illinois
536 South Clark Street
Post Office Box 8136
Chicago, IL 60680

Indiana
575 North Pennsylvania Street
Indianapolis, IN 46204

Iowa
210 Walnut Street
Des Moines, IA 50309

Kansas
VA Regional Office and Medical
Center
901 George Washington
Boulevard
Wichita, KS 67211

Kentucky
545 South Third Street
Louisville, KY 40202

Louisiana
701 Loyola Avenue
New Orleans, LA 70113

Maine
VA Medical and Regional Office
Togus, ME 04330

Maryland
31 Hopkins Plaza
Baltimore, MD 21201

Massachusetts
John F. Kennedy Building
Boston, MA 02203

Michigan
477 Michigan Avenue
Detroit, MI 48226

Minnesota
1 Federal Drive
Fort Snelling
St. Paul, MN 55111

Mississippi
1600 Woodrow Wilson Avenue
Jackson, MS 39269

Missouri
Federal Building
400 South 18th Street
St. Louis, MO 63103

Montana
VA Regional Office and
Medical Center
Fort Harrison, MT 59636

Nebraska
5631 South 48th Street
Lincoln, NE 68516

New Hampshire
275 Chestnut Street, Room 120
Manchester, NH 03101

New Jersey
20 Washington Place
Newark, NJ 07102

New Mexico
500 Gold Avenue, SW
Post Office Box 0968
Albuquerque, NM 87103

New York
111 West Huron Street
Buffalo, NY 14202

New York
245 West Houston Street
New York, NY 10014

North Carolina
251 North Main Street
Winston-Salem, NC 27155

Ohio
1240 East 9th Street
Cleveland, OH 44199

Oklahoma
125 South Main Street
Muskogee, OK 74401

Oregon
1220 SW Third Avenue
Portland, OR 97204

Pennsylvania
VA Regional Office and
Insurance Center
5000 Wissahickon Avenue
Philadelphia, PA 19101

1000 Liberty Avenue
Pittsburgh, PA 15222

South Carolina
1801 Assembly Street
Columbia, SC 29201

Tennessee
110 9th Avenue, South
Nashville, TN 37203

Texas
6900 Almeda Road
Houston, TX 77030

1 Veterans Plaza
701 Clay Avenue
Waco, TX 76799

Utah
125 South State Street
Salt Lake City, UT 84147

Virginia
210 Franklin Road, SW
Roanoke, VA 24011

Washington
915 Second Avenue
Seattle, WA 98174

West Virginia
640 4th Avenue
Huntington, WV 25701

Wisconsin
5000 West National Avenue
Milwaukee, WI 53295

Puerto Rico
150 Carlos Chardon Avenue
Hato Rey, PR 00918

INDEX

BARRON'S BUSINESS KEYS Each "key" explains approximately 50 concepts and provides a glossary and index. Each book: Paperback, approx. 160 pp., 4³⁄₁₆" x 7", $4.95, $5.95, & $7.95 Can. $6.50, $7.95, $8.50, & $11.50.

Keys for Women Starting or Owning a Business (4609-9)
Keys to Avoiding Probate and Reducing Estate Taxes (4668-4)
Keys to Business and Personal Financial Statements (4622-6)
Keys to Buying Foreclosed and Bargain Homes, 2nd *(1294-5)
Keys to Buying and Owning a Home, 3rd Edition *(1299-6)
Keys to Buying and Selling a Business (4430-4)
Keys to Conservative Investments, 2nd Edition (9006-3)
Keys to Improving Your Return on Investments (ROI) (4641-2)
Keys to Incorporating, 2nd Edition (9055-1)
Keys to Investing in Common Stocks, 3rd Edition *(1301-1)
Keys to Investing in Corporate Bonds (4386-3)
Keys to Investing in Government Securities, 2nd Edition (9150-7)
Keys to Investing in International Stocks (4759-1)
Keys to Investing in Municipal Bonds (9515-4)
Keys to Investing in Mutual Funds, 3rd Edition (9644-4)
Keys to Investing in Options and Futures, 3rd Edition *(1303-8)
Keys to Investing in Real Estate, 3rd Edition *(1295-3)
Keys to Investing in Your 401(K), 2nd Edition *(1298-8)
Keys to Managing Your Cash Flow (4755-9)
Keys to Mortgage Financing and Refinancing, 2nd Edition (1436-7)
Keys to Personal Financial Planning, 2nd Edition (1919-9)
Keys to Personal Insurance (4922-5)
Keys to Purchasing a Condo or a Co-op, 2nd Edition *(1305-4)
Keys to Reading an Annual Report, 2nd Edition (9240-6)
Keys to Retirement Planning, 2nd Edition (9013-6)
Keys to Risks and Rewards of Penny Stocks (4300-6)
Keys to Saving Money on Income Taxes, 2nd Edition (9012-8)
Keys to Starting a Small Business (4487-8)
Keys to Starting an Export Business (9600-2)
Keys to Surviving a Tax Audit (4513-0)
Keys to Understanding the Financial News, 3rd Edition *(1308-9)
Keys to Understanding Securities, 2nd Edition *(1309-7)

Available at bookstores, or by mail from Barron's. Enclose check or money order for full amount plus sales tax where applicable and 18% for postage & handling (minimum charge $5.95). Prices subject to change without notice. $= U.S. dollars • Can. $= Canadian dollars • Barron's ISBN Prefix 0-8120, *indicates 0-7641

Barron's Educational Series, Inc.
250 Wireless Boulevard • Hauppauge, NY 11788
In Canada: Georgetown Book Warehouse
34 Armstrong Avenue, Georgetown, Ont. L7G 4R9
www.barronseduc.com   (#10) R 9/00